The Street-wise Popular Practical Guides

The Street-wise Popular Practical Guides

The Street-wise Guide to Buying, Improving, and Selling Your Home

Georgina Burnett

The Home Genie

EER
Edward Everett Root, Publishers, Brighton, 2019.

EER

Edward Everett Root, Publishers, Co. Ltd.,
30 New Road, Brighton, Sussex, BN1 1BN, England.
www.eerpublishing.com

edwardeverettroot@yahoo.co.uk

Details of our overseas agents are given on our website.

First published in Great Britain in 2019.
© Georgina Burnett, 2019.
This edition © Edward Everett Root 2019.

The Street-wise Guide to Buying, Improving, and Selling Your Home.
Georgina Burnett
The Street-wise Popular Practical Guides, no.5.

ISBN 978-1-911454-02-1 Paperback
ISBN 978-1-911454-04-5 Hardback
ISBN 978-1-011454-06-9 eBook

Front cover photograph © Alan Wilson.
All other professional photographs
© Veronica Rodriguez & Nick Henley.

Cover design and typesetting by Head & Heart Book Design.
Printed in Great Britain by TJI Limited, Padstow, Cornwall.

The Street-wise Popular Practical Guides

Edited by Karol Sikora and John Spiers

This original paperback series provides *practical*, expert, insider-knowledge.

Each book tells you what professionals know, but which is not often shared with the public at large.

The books provide vital insider guidance, including what some authorities would prefer you never to know.

The authors are all internationally acknowledged professional experts and skilled popular writers.

We will be pleased to receive suggestions for other titles.

AVAILABLE.

Tom Balchin, *The Street-wise Guide to Surviving a Stroke.*

Eamonn Butler, *The Street-wise Guide to the British Economy.*

Robert Lefever, *The Street-wise Guide to Coping with and Recovering from Addiction.*

Karol Sikora, *The Street-wise Patient's Guide To Surviving Cancer. How to be an active, organised, informed, and welcomed patient.*

Gill Steel, *The Street-wise Guide to Getting the Best From Your Lawyer.*

Lady Teviot, *The Street-wise Guide to Doing Your Family History.*

FORTHCOMING.

Sam Collins, *The Street-wise Guide to Choosing a Care Home.*

Stephen Davies, *The Street-wise Guide to the Devil and His Works*

Raj Persaud and Peter Bruggen, *The Street-wise Guide to Getting the Best Mental Health Care. How to Survive the Mental Health System and Get Some Proper Help.*

Nung Rudarakanchana, *The Street-wise Woman's Guide to Getting The Best Healthcare.*

To Andy, Bonnie and Dexter

Contents

Part 3 SELLING YOUR HOME

The author

Georgina Burnett, aka 'The Home Genie', has been renovating and developing flats and houses for the past decade whilst freelancing as a BBC weather presenter. She also helps others to do the same in her role as a Home Coach. Her vlog and blog TheHomeGenie.com broadcasts entertaining 'how to' videos for property, DIY and general interior styling projects, attracting hundreds of thousands of views. Georgina regularly writes expert comments for *The Sunday Times*, *The Sunday Telegraph*, *The Guardian*, *The Sun*, *The Independent* and numerous interiors magazines. Her passion for DIY makes her the ideal ambassador for both the charity Groundwork UK and BHETA's National Home Improvement Month. She's a presenter for Grand Designs Live, Ideal Home Show and UK Interior Awards and makes guest appearances on the Martin Roberts Talk Radio show.

'Georgina's talent for renovation is evident in each of the properties she has updated and improved. She has a natural flair for design that's backed by a depth of knowledge and experience in the property market, project management and budgeting. This book is a great source of information and inspiration for anyone wanting to transform an unloved property into a desirable home.'
Karen Stylianides, Editor of *Grand Designs Magazine*

'Best blogger for upcycling.' *Daily Mail*

'The Australian-born TV presenter may look eternally glamorous, but she's always ready to get her hands dirty and renovate a house — and the worse it is when she buys it, the better. Georgina has attracted a huge following for her vlogs about how anyone can transform their home themselves.' *Metro*

'Georgina Burnett loves a challenge.' *25 Beautiful Homes Magazine*

'Georgina's personal experience of numerous renovations, her flair for style and her intelligent approach to home improvement whilst sticking to a budget provides a valuable guide to anyone looking to not only get on that property ladder but to climb it rapidly.'
Adam Hollioake, ex-England cricketer and property developer

Thank yous!

I'd like to say sorry and thank you here! Sorry to my abused family that I added just the small task of writing a book to our already hectic schedule. Sorry to my friends for not being there enough during this time and thanks for not totally writing me off! Thanks to John Spiers for approaching me to write a book – without you I certainly wouldn't have entertained the thought for quite some years and to Leigh for holding my hand through the process. Thanks to Doug Reynolds (DJ Reynolds Ltd) for always being on hand for help and advice on just about everything. I must also credit Darren Gibbons (Brewers), Andrew Thomas (Mayflower Solicitors), Mark Stroud (Prospect Financial Ltd) and Tim Wordsworth (Wordsworth Surveyors Ltd) for helping me to make sure all information I was passing onto my lovely readers was present and correct! If it weren't for Sean O'Connell we wouldn't have many of the wonderful photos by Veronica Rodriguez, so thank you to both of you. Thank you also Neil Whitman for your wonderful creative input for the cover.

To my family in particular though, I can't tell you how much I appreciate your support. Nanna your encouragement to achieve has always driven me. Mum and Alan you are just consistently by my side, even when I don't show anywhere near the appropriate amount of gratitude. Dexter the cat, your calming influence as I type must have saved the laptop from being thrown out of the window several times. My darling Bonnie, you won't understand this until you're older, but you're a truly special little person who gives me immense joy. You have put up with not having my full attention with pure grace. Of course, this wouldn't have been possible without my rock Andy, who endures far more than any husband should ever have to as his wife embarks on yet another project. Thank you for being there and not rolling your eyes too many times – well, in front of me anyway!

Introduction

This book is for anyone who is looking to get on and climb the property ladder – even if you think it may not be possible for you.

It's also helpful if you're buying, letting, improving or selling your home.

- It will enable you to be street-wise in the biggest investment you are probably ever going to make.
- I have rented, bought, renovated and sold properties, and I draw on this extensive experience.
- Every key property issue – such as why and when to buy, and getting a mortgage, and insurance – is covered carefully.
- The book is as up-to-date as it has been possible to make it.
- If you are a first-time buyer it should have just about everything you need to know.
- If you just want to buy in a savvy way and improve your home so that you can enjoy it for as long as it fits your lifestyle, this book is relevant.
- It will even be suitable for you if you think that you will never be able to afford to buy your own home. I've included some typical sums to show how you can move from the rental to the home-owning market.
- If you already own property, or have done so in the past, this strategy for moving on up will still work for you.
- If you are selling, the book offers street-wise advice on how to do so in the most cost-effective ways.
- As tax-laws, government policies and markets change it gives guidance to recommended links to find the most up-to-date information online.
- Of course, neither I as the author or my publisher can take any responsibility for actions taken, either by the reader, their family members, or an adviser as a result of reading this book. However, the greatest care has been taken to responsibly provide accurate and up-to-date information here. Whatever you decide to do in the property market you should always take appropriate legal advice.

'The average first-time buyer is now seven years older than in 1960' according to survey results published by *The Independent* in 2018. In 1960 the average buyer was 23, whereas now we are 30. What it didn't point out was the difference in lifestyle, and more importantly expenditure on luxuries.

My concern about reports like this is that anyone reading them is given more of an incentive to lick their imaginary wounds and say 'oh well I might as well not bother', instead of being inventive and finding ways to jump out of the statistic box and into their first home. That's why I have written this book. My approach is optimistic, positive, and go-getting, but also realistic for many!

The media have bombarded us with negative messages about getting on the housing ladder for years. It's not surprising that many think their chances to get on, or indeed climb up, the housing ladder are non-existent. I'm here to help people realise that that simply *isn't* the case for everyone.

So in this book I use my experience, and experience of others I've worked with, to give practical and realistic hints and tips to make the 'unachievable' become perfectly achievable. Yes, it requires some hard work, and some tough choices and it's not an overnight recipe for success...but with a few lifestyle changes and some knowhow about how to maximise your wealth, and the value in your property, I show how it is very possible to not only buy a home, but in time buy the home of your dreams, to improve it as you wish, and to sell it successfully when you want to.

Why am I writing this?

I live in a 7-bedroom house in one of the most expensive areas of the UK, which makes it one of the most expensive towns in the world. I am not saying this to brag. That really isn't my style, I hope. How about I tell you that just nine years ago I bought a property for the first time? That I had just finished a spate of moving 12 times in eight years, going from one rental place to another? That my husband and I have done this by working hard in our jobs, being frugal with our spending and using any spare

''Before' and' after' photos of my latest project

time we have had to do up our homes? The bank of mum and dad was not available to us.

I had thought about buying years beforehand. I had discussed it with a previous boyfriend. He was scared (not sure if it was the commitment of the mortgage or of being tied to me!). Family members warned me off, as they felt it wasn't a good time to buy. I discussed with a friend at great length the possibility of buying together. It never happened. The truth of the matter is, there were many ways I could have got on the property ladder if I'd just thought a bit harder and differently about it. I should have done as well. I can't look back and regret things now though. Luckily when I did buy I bought well and ended my period of procrastination.

It's been hard work. There has nearly been a divorce. But overall I'm pretty much set up for life because of my attitude to my 'homes' over the years. A battered old Ford Focus (the only car we own) still sits in the drive of my 7-bedroom house though, by the way. There's a good reason for that, which I'll tell you about later. All of this is why I wanted to write this book. I felt the need to make sure that you don't just believe the media when they say you can't afford to get on the property ladder and glide up it quickly, as actually I don't believe the statistics tell the whole story.

It's harder than it's ever been to get your first home, of course it is. We could whinge that it's the fault of the government, bankers, landlords, international property investors: the list goes on. Whilst we sit there stewing over these thoughts though, that housing ladder is just getting steeper. It *was* easier for previous generations, but there was also a different attitude to the luxuries in life. These days we mistake luxuries for necessities. In the '60s the average person didn't *need* the latest iPhone and the monthly bill that came with it. They didn't *need* a new TV before the old one died, just because it wasn't big enough anymore. They didn't *need* to wear the latest fashion, no matter the price tag. They didn't dine out regularly, holiday abroad, change their car every time it was close to being embarrassing. Now I'm not saying that if everyone saw these 'necessities' for what they really are it would solve the housing crisis in the UK. I am totally aware that many can't even afford them in the first place. I am saying that our modern priorities and spending habits do not work in our favour when it comes to being able to afford a home.

This book is not a silver bullet. I'm sad to say there are many out there who still won't be able to own their own property because of circumstances beyond their control. I will continue to try and help these communities in any way I can, which is why I became an ambassador for Groundwork UK. It's an amazing charity that works with the most disadvantaged communities in the UK. They help people to create better environments, to improve their prospects and to live and work in a greener way. Groundwork also teaches DIY skills to encourage recycling, which is a theme that you will notice pops up a lot in this book! I like to support them not only because I truly believe in what they do, but because although I don't 'come from money' I do know that I have been lucky enough to be in the right place at the right time, with the right attitude – a lot! What this book will do though, is help you to put yourself in the right place at the right time, but most importantly with the right attitude.

There are many more of you out there who can do what I've done. Please make sure you truly understand which category you come under. It's very easy to adopt the attitude of 'poor me' when there is more within your circle of control than you choose to accept (oh I'm a life coach as well, by the way!). I warn you though that it needs to be more of a priority in your life. You probably won't be following in your parents' footsteps. It won't necessarily be easy, and will be challenging. Your first few homes probably won't be the ones you dreamt of when you were growing up – far from it. However, I believe that you can, and will, get there in time.

If none of what I've talked about appeals to you then please put the book down now, rent for the rest of your life, but accept that you made that choice. Not that that's a bad thing. In many European countries that is the norm. They don't have a problem with not owning their home and therefore don't stress about it. That's fine. But if you could have followed this guidance and you chose not to, please be happy about that decision and don't look back.

I've designed this book for first-time buyers so it has everything you need to know about buying, improving and selling a property. But if you are already a homeowner or have been in the past, you will still benefit from my experience – you will just already be that bit further ahead, so lucky you. It has all the minutiae you need to know, but I also give you my life coaching tips to make sure you get through this in the most positive way. Even more importantly you can learn from my insider-tips I've picked up over the years, which will give you a powerful new approach to buying, improving and selling your home.

If you want to read more about my background and what has motivated me in my life, jump to the 'About the Author' section at the end. For those of you still here, let's crack on!

PART ONE

BUYING YOUR HOME

CHAPTER 1:
Why and when to buy

Exit plan

It might seem strange to start a book with an exit plan, but hindsight is a wonderful thing. I should, and could, have bought a property a lot earlier than I did. I simply didn't have the courage, but people feeding my fears also surrounded me. What if I didn't have enough work and couldn't pay the mortgage? What if I needed to move away and was stuck because of my property? What if, what if, what if?!

What I should have been asking was: what if, apart from a few blips, property prices continue to rise and I miss out on the best investment I could ever make? What if I spend the next ten years paying off my landlord's mortgage with nothing to show for it at the end? Unfortunately, that's what my fears actually led to.

So if you are going through this same dilemma ask yourself the following questions and write the answers down.

- What will happen if I buy a property?
- What won't happen if I buy a property?
- What will happen if I don't buy a property?
- What won't happen if I don't buy a property?

If you are still asking 'what if' then let's go through some rational answers. I am trying to think of all the possible questions you are going to be asking here. If I've missed anything out let me know so I can get it into the revised edition of this book!

- What if I don't have enough work and couldn't pay the mortgage?
- What if I lose my job?
- What if my business goes bust?
- What if I, or my partner, get pregnant?
- What if I need to move away and am stuck because of my property?

- What if I want to go off travelling?
- What if I want to study (or go back to studying)?
- What if I meet someone and the place isn't big enough for us?
- What if my parents fall ill and I need to look after them?
- What if I fall ill or have an accident and can't work?
- What if I have kids, but I don't live in the right catchment area for schools?
- What if my work moves?
- What if interest rates increase?
- What if house prices fall?
- What if I die?!

Obviously I tried to come up with some answers too. Different people will pair different answers with different questions as they are all essentially trying to tackle the same thing, and it's all about what makes you feel most comfortable:

✓ Rent your place out and rent somewhere bigger/more affordable/in the right location. Yes you are wasting money on rent still, but someone else is helping to contribute to the capital gain of the property you own (this is a very different ball game to renting without your own property in the picture).

✓ Get a lodger.

✓ Airbnb your room and sleep in the lounge.

✓ Sell (although often not the most savvy decision in the long run)

✓ Wait for house prices to rise again, as history strongly suggests they will.

✓ Rent your house out during the time you need to be in the right catchment area and rent closer to the school.

✓ Look into insurance to cover the principal concern you have (again, this has a cost associated with it, so make sure you're only doing the absolute minimum you need to feel comfortable).

If it still doesn't feel right, then I surrender, but at least I feel satisfied you will have explored this thoroughly first! It may simply be that buying a house is not for you, either now…or indeed ever!

When is the best time to buy?

Well there are a couple of aspects to this. There is the best market to buy in, and the best time personally. Of course the law of sod means these rarely coincide! The perfect combination would be:

✓ The housing market has hit rock bottom.
✓ It's a buyer's market. This is when there are more people wanting to sell than buy property.
✓ You have saved a sizeable deposit.
✓ Your income is stable and is likely to remain so in the coming years.
✓ You are flexible about where you live.
✓ You are not expecting a baby any time soon (more about this later).
✓ You don't have a property to sell (surprised by this? Again, more on this later).

Even if you can't tick all these boxes, that's not always a reason to hold back. The following is a bit more realistic and a list to aspire to as your ground zero:

The housing market is not at its top level
If this is your first rung on the ladder and you're buying at the height of market, you might as well spread butter on the rungs above. It's reasonable to expect a property to increase in value over time – history has borne this out. If you buy when it's at the very top of the market, however, it will be harder for you to see that increase, and therefore climb to the next rung. Unless you pick up an absolute bargain, there won't be enough of a margin to move up to the next property comfortably.

You may think, 'well what does it matter as I'm expecting to stay here for the rest of my life'? I'm afraid that 'life' sometimes pans out differently to what we expect, so you have to prepare for the worst. Working out where the market is can be done with some due diligence using tools like Zoopla. Yes, talking to agents can help, but remember they want to sell so aren't always your most discerning of informants. The media can also help, but again they are looking for headlines and what affects one area of the market doesn't necessarily affect the whole market. Zoopla, Rightmove and others all give you access to local information that helps you make an informed decision based on independent data.

Yes your exit plan should cover the bad times, but if you've bought at a particularly high price you may find that if you have to move and rent your property out that the rent won't cover the mortgage payments.

You have a reasonable deposit saved

'Reasonable' of course means 'enough' for what you want to buy. I'd say as soon as you have enough to buy a property with the criteria I will divulge in following chapters, it's 'reasonable' – as don't forget that whilst you're saving, property prices are usually also rising. One thing to bear in mind here though is that the more you're looking to borrow for a property, the bigger the effect a difference in interest rates can make, and so it will sometimes be well worth trying to take your deposit from 18% of the value to 20% of the value where you'll usually catch yourself a better deal.

Your income is fairly stable

On this point though, your exit plan should cover the potential bad times, as discussed earlier.

You can be reasonably flexible about where you live within a region

This just helps you to have more of a market to cover.

You are not expecting a baby in the immediate future

When I was expecting my first baby I took on a derelict 7-bedroom house to renovate, so am I the best person to give advice on this? Hell yeah! Let me tell you why. In my NCT group, every single person was moving, extending or renovating their home. This is so common. It's human nature that we leave things until the last minute. In our case, we didn't actually need to move. We had a sufficiently big enough house, but our fears were that it was getting close to the next tier of stamp duty, which would then cause problems when we came to sell. We were basing this on a nearly identical property opposite, that had just sold. It actually

Me scraping walls with my family when 5 months pregnant!

turned out to be way over that threshold (the property opposite had been undersold) but because we got an offer within four days of putting it on the market we decided to press on.

We couldn't find a suitable property to buy, so when our buyer was trying to bring down the price we pointed out that actually we were in no hurry to sell. They were in a hurry to buy though. They were coming from a one bedroom flat in London. They had a buyer and were expecting a baby very soon. We decided that if they were prepared to pay top market value, then we would suck it up, sell and rent for a while. This way we could have our baby and look when we weren't in a hurry and would be a more desirable chain-free buyer. It turned out that we found the derelict doer-upper (a far bigger project than we had set out to buy, I might add) just in time. There was no rush though as we would need to rent anyway whilst doing this up.

Let's look at the difference between us and the other couple as it's a real lesson in how to do well in property:

Us	Them
Expecting a child	Expecting a child
Wanting to be near station	Wanting to be near station
Happy to stay at current property if necessary	Wanting to move in before baby arrived
After a doer-upper	After a recently refurbished (and therefore top of market) property
Happy to rent if necessary	In property that would be too small once baby arrived
In no hurry	In a tearing hurry!

I'm very sorry to say (and I genuinely mean that) that they came to sell three years later at the point of expecting their second child (yep, they did the same again) and couldn't achieve the price they bought it for as the market dropped.

The hard work in the house we sold them had definitely fallen on our shoulders though. We had lived in rubble and dust whilst we extended and had the kitchen and bathroom replaced. We worked on the house every evening and weekend – sanding floors, decorating, painting spindles, staining floorboards, the list goes on. We had to move twice because we rented whilst doing up the next place. We also had to renovate the next property with a baby in tow.

Financially, we have definitely been the winners here, but yes we have also put in more effort and hours. We sacrificed the 'dream' of living in the perfectly finished home when having a baby. We did make a mistake though. Our mistake was waiting until I was pregnant to make the move. To be fair, we weren't looking for a project this time, but ended up with our biggest yet! It was no fun doing one of that size when coping with the shock of having a new-born. It would have been worse if we had rushed into buying the wrong place at the right time though. The moral of this story is 'think ahead'. Don't wait until crunch-time to get nesting.

Of course I accept that you may be massaging your bump as you read this, wailing into your sleeve. Life isn't perfect, and so plan B is to definitely not let your vendor (and estate agent) know you are pregnant as this will put them in the driving seat. Whatever you do, don't buy in a rush. If you can't find what you're looking for then cram that cot into your current place and start looking when the fog of sleepless nights clears.

Finally, plan C. If you find the right place and the timing is too close to comfort for D-Day, and you fear you may be heaving removal boxes in between contractions, could you afford to rent for a couple of months so you're not moving in the middle of it all? Or do you have relatives you could stay with to smooth things over and make sure you're not rushed into a sale you will come to regret? Coming up with other plans is all about being a chilled, savvy buyer. It is about letting go of the 'dream' in the near future and all about going after the long-term goal. Trust me it will be worth it.

CHAPTER 2:
Preparing to Buy

Getting a deposit together

I'm not a big fan of the whole keeping up with the Joneses thing. I think it must be exhausting when I can see that someone is looking over their shoulder at what others have. What I find even more irritating is the judgment that comes with which handbag you carry, which car you drive, where you holiday. When I rock up in my 57 reg Ford Focus, that I bought second-hand seven years ago when the previous second-hand car gave up the ghost, can you imagine what they think? They're certainly surprised when they see my house as people often think the flashy car should come first. Equally though, killing yourself to cover a massive mortgage just so you can impress people with your square footage also doesn't make sense. Your property should fit financially for you and that means working your way gradually to the ideal home, rather than relying on mortgaging yourself up to the eyeballs.

Credit is great when used wisely, but it should never be used to better our image. In the long run that attitude will not serve us well. 'But I just like the nicer things in life' you say. I urge you to evaluate your straw house lifestyle, which is ready to fall down at the whisper of a wind.

Let's talk about Mr and Mrs average earner (statistically speaking)

Between them they earn £53,000

They spend:
Food and essentials £3,000
Mobile phone bill £880
Weekly travel £8,400
Rent £11,000
Monthly utilities and council tax bills £3,900

These are all statistics that I have found to be the average from various sources and of course they will all differ massively from household to household. But if these figures are to be believed, saving a deposit for a house for Mr and Mrs Average should not be impossible, in fact not even difficult. I use Mr and Mrs Average, because I appreciate that there are many families living on the breadline who can only dream about having that kind of income. I'm talking to those of you who do earn at least close to an average salary, but spend in a way that will of course prevent you from getting on the property ladder.

You will notice I don't include holidays, eating or drinking out, clothes and other purchases. You may be screaming at me saying it's unrealistic, but remember this is just in the short term. It may seem unworkable in today's current mind-set, but when the media report that average earners can't afford to get on the property ladder it is not always true of Mr and Mrs Average. Results from a survey published by the *Telegraph* showed that Brits spend an average of £1,042 on clothes per year. Do clothes fall apart that quickly that we need to spend £90 per month on replacing them? Or have we become conditioned to spend rather than save? The truth is that the priorities are no longer the same. If buying a house was that important we would buy second-hand clothes, or mend and make do – that is the big difference between home buyers in the '60s and now. Our throwaway culture is part of the property problem.

Very few people *need* the latest phone, an impressive car, an expensive holiday, the latest fashion, even designer dogs! Yes it's desirable, but to me the security bricks and mortar offer is far more desirable. If you truly want to buy, I urge you to look at your outgoings and see where your priorities lie. It may even be that you do have some kind of deposit but could actually get a larger one together once you have done this exercise. Remember the greater your deposit, not only do you have to borrow less, but what you do borrow may well be at a lower interest rate.

Take a look at your bank statements and work out what you spend per month on luxuries. Even better, spend a few weeks writing down every penny that leaves your pocket so you get an in-depth picture of your spending habits. Then decide what you could live without if it meant you could get a deposit (or a bigger deposit) together more quickly. Here are some suggestions for saving money:

✓ Reduce your energy and water use – easier than you might think when you put your mind to it
✓ Rent somewhere cheaper
✓ House-share, or if permitted get another lodger
✓ Only buy second-hand or benefit from sites like Freecycle.org
✓ Mend or make-do with clothes and other items
✓ Sacrifice your daily coffee out
✓ Take a packed lunch to work
✓ Give up drinking anything but tap water
✓ Give up smoking
✓ Become a property guardian and pay zero rent
✓ Move in with family
✓ Agree to meet up with friends for walking get-togethers rather than at a bar or restaurant – better for the soul, waistline and the property fund!
✓ Swap skills – what could you do in return for haircuts, for example?
✓ DIY hair and beauty treatments
✓ Car share to work (worked out pretty well for Peter Kay!)
✓ Arrange to work from home more often to cut down travel costs
✓ Manipulate your working hours so you're not travelling during peak hours
✓ Swap holidays abroad for camping or Airbnb staycations
✓ Walk more to reduce your petrol and parking bills

Remember this is not forever. Visualise the home you can own at the end of this to keep you going when you're finding it hard. Keep a log of what you're saving by making any of these lifestyle changes so you have something tangible to show for your efforts. Once you are in the habit of scaling back it's amazing how that stays with you. That can only be a good thing to take the pressure off when you are committed to monthly mortgage payments right? It also really makes you appreciate what you do have.

Borrowing money from family

Of course we hear about how many people rely on the bank of mum and dad. That's nothing new though. If you're lucky enough to have access to that bank then use this fortune wisely and it's still worth making lifestyle changes to build as much of a deposit as possible as you will have more choice and possibly pay lower mortgage rates. If mum and dad are reluctant to help you out, but can afford to, it might be worth explaining the strategy in this book so they can see you have a wise plan in place. If you do your sums it may be possible to work out a repayment plan over time. Put together a contract so you all know where you stand!

Credit rating

When you first start thinking about buying your home you need to know what state your credit file is in. You can usually get a free trial online to do this (remember to cancel though if you don't want to continue subscribing). All credit bureaus have to offer a statutory report for just a couple of pounds as well, and at the time of writing this, Money Saving Expert also has a free credit club. You want to make sure the information on your file is accurate. Don't check your credit rating too many times in short succession though as that can then go against your record! It's also important to know that lenders credit score in different ways so just because a bureau says you have a high rating, it doesn't guarantee a mortgage will be offered by all lenders.

Here are a number of ways you can improve your credit rating:
- ✓ Get on the electoral role. This is a really simple one and an absolute must.
- ✓ The longer you stay at an address the better your rating tends to be too.
- ✓ Keep a bank account for as long as possible.
- ✓ Become independent. If you are financially associated with anyone from the past, via a mortgage or bank account, for example, their financial situation could have an impact on your rating so you need to let credit reference agencies know that you are no longer linked.

✓ Take out a credit card if you haven't one already as it helps to have a credit history. You need to use this card too. I don't mean go out and spend money for the sake of it, but do use it for essentials you would be buying anyway. Make sure you set up a standing order though and budget so you can pay it off each month. Paying more than the minimum amount goes in your favour, and we also don't want to be accruing debt when we are looking to get a mortgage. If you can't trust yourself with a credit card then just make a couple of small payments a month using it so it's easier to pay off as you go.

✓ Close any credit cards you no longer use. When you have credit cards open but don't use them it has a negative effect on your rating. The same goes for store cards and mobile phone contracts.

✓ Pay your bills on time. It's not just late credit card payments that affect your credit score, but also missed or late payments for utilities bills. It's worth setting up direct debits for these.

✓ Use a prepaid card to build credit. There is a nominal monthly fee for this for 12 months, but you don't require a credit reference. At the end it will be added to your credit file that you have repaid a debt.

What can you afford?

Assuming we have our deposit together it's time to get cracking. You need to make sure you are very clear on your financial situation.

Your deposit is not all of the spare money you have saved. You will need 1% of the purchase price to cover fees and moving costs. This should conservatively allow for any necessary surveys, solicitor's fees and moving day expenses and you may have to consider stamp duty too. If you follow my lead you will also need money for improvements so take this into account. It could be possible to get a loan to help you out with that though, or you could stagger the improvements as you save. But it should still be a consideration when working out what you can afford to pay for a property.

Stamp Duty

Stamp Duty Land Tax, as it's officially known, has to be paid on properties above a certain price in England, Wales and Northern Ireland. It currently differs according to whether you (or the person you are buying with) are a first-time buyer or not. It will adversely affect how much you pay if you also own another residential property.

If you don't currently own a property, but have done in the past you do not get the same privileges as a complete newbie to the ladder. Of course all this is subject to change, but at the time of writing this, first-time buyers are exempt from paying on properties below £300,000 and benefit from lower rates above that.

For a stamp duty calculator you can go to:
www.tax.service.gov.uk/calculate-stamp-duty-land-tax
www.stampdutycalculator.org.uk
www.moneyadviceservice.org.uk/en/tools/house-buying/stamp-duty-calculator
www.moneysavingexpert.com/mortgages/stamp-duty

By the way, stamp duty is due within 30 days of completion. Your solicitor or agent will often sort this out on the day of completion and add the amount to their bill, but it is your responsibility to make sure it is done.

First time buyer incentives

If you are a first-time buyer, or you have owned before and can't afford to buy now, there are some incentives offered by the government.

As these could change at any time, it's best that I only give you a brief overview so you are at least aware of what might be available. Also I want to point out things to consider, so you're not seeing the options through rose-tinted glasses.

According to MoneySuperMarket and Country and Living stats, at the end of 2017 the government's 'Help To Buy' scheme had seen the number of first-time buyers at its highest level since the financial crisis in 2008.

There are a few ways this has helped struggling buyers. For example in England if your household earnings are under the threshold there's a government-backed equity loan scheme that covers up to 20% of the cost of a property. So you will only need a 5% deposit with a 75% mortgage. You won't be charged interest on the loan for the first five years of owning the property. You will still be paying interest on the mortgage of course. At the time of writing this, it's only applicable to new-build homes and is different for Wales, Scotland and London. There are also further incentives if you are serving in the armed forces.

The government will boost your savings if you invest in a Help to Buy: ISA and there's also the Shared Ownership option. You basically buy a share (between 25% and 75%) of the home's value and pay rent on the remaining share. You can buy bigger shares later if you can afford it. Here you are restricted to new-builds or a property being sold by housing associations. Shared ownership properties will always be leasehold until you own 100% of the property.

It is definitely worth going to www.helptobuy.gov.uk to find out what the latest scheme is offering, but do the sums fully to work out what you're entering into as there are potential pitfalls. For example, you are restricted to a certain market and even certain developers. I'll go into this in more detail later in the book, but new-builds tend to be more expensive and history says they don't rise in value as quickly. With the loan, although you don't pay interest on it for the first five years, and you should have a competitive rate after that, the amount is not fixed. It will become increasingly expensive. Whilst you should be able to get your hands on cheaper mortgage rates if you go down this route, it will only be with certain lenders so you won't have access to the whole market.

There is also a Starter Homes scheme coming, only applicable to England. First-time buyers can benefit from a 20% discount on certain new-builds up to a certain value. Although at the time of writing this it hasn't launched yet, you can register your interest at www.ownyourhome.gov.uk/scheme/starter-homes/

I think my biggest concern about buying through these schemes is that with future governments, fees and terms could change and you will be at their mercy.

As I mentioned before though, it is worth knowing your options and speaking to a 'whole of market' mortgage adviser so you are going in with your eyes open. Always work out the sums for the worst-case scenario so you know where you stand.

Buying with a friend

If you're strapped for cash, or want to move on up that ladder quickly it might make sense to buy with a friend. You can pool your money together, share the workload of making any improvements and then split the bills once you're living there.

I talked about the stats comparing current first-time buyers with those in the '60s in my introduction. One of the interesting factors was how many more of those were married in comparison with today's house-hunters. This will probably have a bearing on the age at which people buy too. I know that I felt quite free-spirited when I was single and it wasn't until I met my now husband and felt more settled that I seriously thought about laying down roots. We are getting married and having children much later in life, if at all, these days. But buying a home should not necessarily be dependent on that relationship security. If you're going to rent a flat-share with someone, why not both benefit from the financial incentives of owning together instead.

If you do go down this route you need to make sure it is with someone you can communicate with and who is likely to help with the workload when it comes to improvements and upkeep. You may even be able to come to an understanding that one person is providing funds whilst the other does all the grunt work. Anything that you do decide needs to be written down in a contract. It also makes sense to plan what will happen if one of you wants to sell before the other – or even set a date for this. Don't forget that if you have bought and improved a property sensibly it should have gone up in value so in the right market you will still be better off than if you had carried on renting.

Partnering with an investor

You may be able to find an investor who wants to buy with you to share the cost of improvements and rent the other room or rooms out. The best place to meet someone like this is at a property networking evening. You should be able to find local events with a quick Internet search. They usually tend to be a friendly bunch in my experience, but it would still be wise to get some professional advice when entering into an agreement. For one thing if they are renting out rooms it will affect the kind of mortgage you can go for. An investor is likely to be more experienced than you, so you want to make sure you are getting a fair deal. Again everything should be in a contract – don't ever be tempted to go with a handshake – no matter how good the deal!

To do list

- Write down all your fears and come up with solutions
- Look at your outgoings and see where your money is being spent
- Work out which changes you could make to save money
- Decide on the amount you want to save and set a deadline
- Come up with a reasonable budget to achieve that goal
- Write your commitment to sticking to that budget
- Check your credit rating and make any necessary changes to improve it
- Estimate how much you will need to put aside for fees and moving day costs
- Check out your eligibility for any first-time buyer incentives and understand what that will mean in the long term
- Estimate how much stamp duty (if any) you need to budget for
- Chat to friends and family about the possibility of buying together (give them this book to read!)
- Attend a local property investors networking evening

CHAPTER 3:
Getting a mortgage

Mortgages AAAAARGH!

It's now time to talk to a mortgage adviser to find out the lay of the land. Not everybody will feel that they need to do this, but if it's your first time I recommend it as a starting point. If you are more confident and knowledgeable though, the information available to you on the Internet is vast, with comparison sites doing a lot of the hard work for you so you can skip this bit. The rest of you, bear with me as this is possibly the most boring bit of this entire book – but it is essential information!

Notice we are doing this before we even start looking at where or what we are buying! Let's face it, you wouldn't go to the Aston Martin dealership unless you knew you had the money to buy one or the ability to get one on credit (unless you like a cheeky test drive!). So let's work out what we can afford before we even think of going shopping.

The truth of the matter is that if you are thinking of buying, you won't have been able to stop yourself from scanning online or shimmying past an estate agent's window. So you probably have a rough idea. I always think it's best not to get your heart set on an ideal property in an ideal location before you know you can even get close to affording it comfortably. This is likely to be the most you've ever spent on anything, so you need your wits about you. If you've ever been in love with anything or anyone you will know the silly decisions you can tend to make under the spell. Trust me, house love is the most bewitching of all and can cost you dearly! Yes, speaking to a mortgage adviser can help you to know how much you need to save for a deposit, but remember whilst you're saving, house prices could very well be increasing too.

What you need before speaking to a mortgage adviser or broker

To save everyone's time it's worth getting the following information together before you even pick up the phone to a mortgage adviser or broker:

- How much available cash you have. Remember to point out this will need to include any fees, moving costs and stamp duty – let them do the sums!
- Your average incomings and outgoings. Your bank statements for the past three months should be sufficient. This should be looking healthier after our earlier exercise of course!
- Your salary details, if you are employed. So payslips and your most recent P60
- Self-assessment tax return
- Your employment history
- If you are self-employed you need your business accounts from the past two years, although some lenders are willing to lend based on one year's trading. Warning: mortgage options tend to be more limited unless you have a strong track record.
- A passport or driving licence for proof of identity.
- A utility bill for proof of address.
- Your address history
- Employment history
- 3 months of bank statements
- Credit card balances
- Any other credit commitments/outstanding balances

At the very initial stages they won't need to see the above and will just take the figures from you. Wouldn't it be better to know you are giving them exact figures though and then when you find the ideal property, everything is all neatly to hand?

It makes sense to have a rough idea of the price of property you're likely to be looking at. It's also worth spending time experimenting with an online mortgage calculator. Try different house prices, deposits and lengths of payment to see what you feel you could comfortably afford.

Consider this as well: if you only need a 1-bedder, could you comfortably stretch to a 2-bedder, perhaps in a less expensive location, potentially allowing you to have a lodger or to Airbnb the spare room? Be conservative in your calculations, and don't expect to have 100% occupancy. This could be a way of future proofing your climb up the ladder. It's worth having done your due diligence on this before you approach the mortgage adviser. Remember though, the higher your deposit, the better the interest rate you're likely to pay.

Remember to say you do not want them to do a credit check, unless you have had a problem with credit and feel you need to know this.

What is a mortgage?

Let's just get the bare bones established, because this isn't taught thoroughly in all schools as far as I know, and yet it's a massive consideration for most adults. 'Paying off the mortgage' is a dream that many have their whole working lives. A mortgage is a loan. You borrow money from a lender for an agreed period and you pay interest on that loan. The norm is 25 years but many lenders will go to 35 or even 40 years to assist affordability. You can switch mortgages before the end of the mortgage life to get better deals, which I will go into more detail on later. If you can't keep up with your monthly payments the lender will then take ownership of the house and the sad fact is you're back to square one, renting, having lost the deposit, any money you've paid into the property, and not benefitting from any increase in value. Although they are common, mortgages are serious business.

How to find a mortgage adviser or broker

So how do you find a mortgage adviser or broker? Well they come in all shapes and sizes. Some have alliances to lenders, some are restricted in the mortgages they can find for you. Ideally you want to find one that is 'whole of market'. This means they will have the biggest variety of deals to show you, so you are more likely to find the one that is most suitable for you.

Some of the ways you could find an adviser or broker are:

By recommendation
You will see this pop up a lot in this book. I always think it's great when you can get anything that has been recommended by someone. But it has to be the right someone. If I want a recommendation for a holiday these days, I'm not going to ask a backpacking student as I don't fancy sharing a bunk-bed and I also value being able to shower every day on holiday... If you know someone you respect that is in a similar situation to you ask them for a recommendation. It's still worth doing your own digging and there's nothing, apart from time, stopping you from speaking to a couple of advisers.

Through an estate agent
You will often find when you speak to estate agents that they ask you if you have a mortgage ready. This is partly because they want to know you are serious, but also because they often have an associated mortgage service. I haven't gone with one of these in the past because I find it a bit of a conflict of interest and like to keep things separate. For a start I don't want to discuss every small detail of my financial situation with anyone connected to the person I may need to negotiate a price down on my behalf!

A colleague of mine was suspicious when he spoke to one about securing a mortgage for £210K and started receiving emails from the associated agent about... £210k properties! Even more coincidental was that when he was then called up to be told he could actually get a mortgage for £250k he started receiving properties to the value of... £250k from the agent! Now of course this isn't going to be the case with all in-house mortgage arrangements, so that is something for you to go with your gut on.

Through a bank or building society
Bear in mind a broker who works for a bank is only going to suggest mortgages offered by that bank or any partners. I would always find one that was offering the whole of the market.

Search online
Just like anything in life these days, it's worth turning to Google. There is an abundance of sites helping you to find the 'best' broker/ adviser locally to you. It's worth scrolling down through a few pages as remember just because a site is at the top of the list, it

just makes them the best at Search Engine Optimisation (SEO), not necessarily the best at what they actually do.

Ask whomever you end up talking with for their 'Initial Disclosure Document'. This will tell you exactly what kind of service you can expect and whether there will be any fees payable to the broker, as not all have their fees covered by the lender.

Of course you don't have to use a mortgage adviser or broker, you could just do the research yourself. This is called an execution-only mortgage. This is not really advisable unless you are very experienced. Remember if you *have* been advised and the mortgage turns out to be unsuitable you can complain to the Financial Ombudsman Service. If you've done it yourself...well you're on your own love! Once you have been advised, however, I'd always double check with some research online in case they missed anything.

Types of mortgage

The different domestic mortgages available are like horses for courses. Your adviser should be able to pick the right kind of mortgage for your particular situation, but it helps if you know what they are before your discussion.

You can decide to do interest-only or repayment. Interest-only means your monthly payments will be lower, but you won't be eating into the actual sum you have borrowed. It's much harder to get this type of mortgage now than it was 10 years ago. It is meant to enable homeowners to invest elsewhere to help them pay off the mortgage at the end of its term. Of course in theory the property should be going up in value over the years so the ratio of the amount you borrowed to the value of the house should be tipping in your favour. Repayment means you will be paying the interest and an agreed amount of the mortgage value each month.

If you can afford it, repayment will enable you to pay off your mortgage more quickly, which is what we all want to do, right? If you need more cash available for say starting up a business, then you may want to do interest-only, but of course you are gambling with your home and security by doing this. If you have a habit of spending more than is necessary, or you've been through your outgoings as I suggested earlier and have found that there are areas where you could be more frugal, committing to repayment will do you a favour IF you can reign in the spending. It may be you need to do interest-only so you can afford to pay for improvements, but always look at every option and the associated cost implications.

The two main types of mortgage are fixed rate and variable rate. You tend to have a deal for an agreed number of years and then it reverts to the lender's standard variable rate, at which point you can find a new deal if you wish.

Fixed rate

The interest rate will stay the same for the duration of the introductory period. This would usually be between one and five years. It then reverts to the lender's standard variable rate for the rest of the mortgage.

Many like the idea of fixed rate because you can plan ahead and will know exactly how much you are paying each month no matter what is happening to the base interest rate set by the Bank of England. If your fixed rate is agreed at the time of low interest rates, you are winning, but if the base rate goes down during your deal period then you won't be able to benefit from the lower interest rates of course.

Variable rate mortgages

Tracker and discounted mortgages come under this banner, but there are many others where the amount of interest you pay on a monthly basis varies.

Tracker

This is linked to the Bank of England base rate and rises and falls respectively. You will be able to take advantage of interest rates falling with this, but it will be hard to plan how much you will be paying each month. At the end of the life of the deal (typically 2, 3 or 5 years) it then reverts to the lender's standard variable rate.

Discounted mortgage

This has a fixed percentage below a specified interest rate, commonly the lender's standard variable rate. This means the interest rate can go up or down.

Offset mortgage

The interest you pay on this mortgage is dependent on how much money you have in your accounts. In other words the more savings you have, the less interest you pay. These savings aren't actually paying off the mortgage, they just help to reduce the amount of interest you pay. The interest rate for this type of mortgage tends to be higher, and you are only likely to benefit from it if you have plenty of cash in the bank. It's worked well for me in the past as I have been freelance for most of my career, so it's been a case of feast or famine rather than a regular monthly income.

You have probably heard the quick garbled message at the end of adverts 'your home will be at risk if you do not keep up repayments'. It's easy to become complacent about this, but I need to reiterate if you can't pay your mortgage, the provider will take your home away. This is why we have our exit plan though, isn't it guys?! It's also worth doing worst-case scenario sums to make sure you can either afford it if interest rates go up, or that your plan B will still work.

Mortgage agreement in principle (AIP)

At this stage, you simply want to know how much of a mortgage you are likely to be able to afford. If you find a property you want and there's competition, you might need to make yourself appear to be a serious buyer and someone who can move quickly. In this instance you might want a 'mortgage agreement in principle'. This is where a very basic assessment of your financial situation is carried out. The lender is saying that 'in principle' you would be able to get a mortgage for 'x' amount. They will need to do a credit check for this and the offer usually only lasts for about 90 days. Beware that if your offer is rejected, along with others over a short period, the multiple credit checks can harm your credit rating.

Agents often like to know you have an AIP as they feel more comfortable spending time with people who can definitely progress when they've had an offer accepted. Doing your homework thoroughly on what you are likely to be able to afford though should give you the confidence to progress.

If you are planning to do a quick turnaround with the property you end up buying, this is something you need to discuss with your broker as you want to make sure you have a mortgage product without an early repayment charge. I go into this in more detail in the 'How To Sell Your Home' section.

Remortgaging

If you are improving your property, the value should increase faster than the market. When you come to the end of your mortgage deal (typically 2-5 years) it can often pay to remortgage to get a better rate than the standard variable rate your current lender is likely to put you on. Even more positive is the fact that because the value of your home has increased rapidly due to improvements made you could be on a lower loan-to-value band so will get a better deal. Start looking into this three to four months before your deal is up. There may be charges for switching though so make sure you do the sums. It also helps to put together a guide for lenders as to why you think the house will have increased in value, including photos, details of improvements made, any positive changes to the area and comparable properties that have sold well recently.

It's really important to remember that the bigger your deposit is, the better (less expensive) the mortgage deal is likely to be. You will probably also pay less stamp duty the cheaper the property. This all needs to be taken into account when working out the type of property you will start hunting for.

To do list

- Use an online mortgage calculator to estimate the value of property you could afford with your deposit
- Get your documents ready for talking to a mortgage adviser/ broker
- Ask friends, colleagues and family for broker recommendations
- Do your own online research into mortgage deals
- Book an appointment with a broker or adviser
- It's also worth starting to get recommendations for conveyancing solicitors at this point in case you need to move quickly

CHAPTER 4:
What type of property and where?

So let's go shopping!!!

Woohoo, thank goodness we are past the mortgage bit and onto my favourite part (trust me it was as hard sitting down long enough to write that chapter as it was for you to read it!).

Now let's have some fun.

Home vision board

This is my favourite bit. I love nothing more than to daydream about how I want something in my life to be. Under duress, my husband did a vision board with me about 10 years ago. He thought the idea was a bit silly but still humoured me as we went about cutting out images from magazines and sticking them on a large sheet of card. Just about every one of those images is now our reality. To put it in perspective, we were renting a 2-bed flat, which was one floor of a converted three-storey Victorian townhouse. The old lady downstairs used to bang on her ceiling with a broom every time we so much as sneezed. The six people living above us worked in bars and restaurants and used to stay up most nights, because presumably they slept all day. The windows rattled when the wind blew or a large vehicle went by. We dreamed of owning an entire house like this, but decorated so it was worthy of being in an interiors magazine.

Well, the first floor of our current three-storey house is very similar to the size of our rented flat at that time and is even on the same road. Our home has been featured in *Metro Home* and *25 Beautiful Homes*. I don't think either of us totally believed we would achieve this within 10 years. Maybe just putting it on our vision board planted enough belief deep down to make it happen. Note that there have been a number of houses in between the rented flat and the 7-bedder. They weren't on my vision board as they were just part of the journey though. So have some fun with this. Grab some interiors magazines, newspapers, or you could just find images online and print them out. I personally like to have at least an A3 piece of card – I always have plenty I want to cram into mine!

Here are some things to think about when looking to create your vision board. For now I'd like you to fill in the details below:

- ✓ Location (even the actual road if you like, but town or village is pretty good)
- ✓ Square footage
- ✓ Number of bedrooms (you may need to think about how many kids, cats or dogs you're planning to have in the future if you're not there yet)
- ✓ Do you have a walk-in wardrobe?
- ✓ Number of bathrooms – is there an ensuite?
- ✓ Number of reception rooms
- ✓ A gym
- ✓ Entrance
- ✓ Is it terraced, semi-detached, detached?
- ✓ Is it a new-build or period property?
- ✓ Is the kitchen open-plan into a diner/lounge or are they separate?
- ✓ Is there a garden, what is it like?
- ✓ Driveway, garage?
- ✓ Colour schemes
- ✓ Furniture
- ✓ What kind of neighbours do you want?

This may seem very detailed for a wish list, but the more you can fit into your head, the more real it becomes. You've heard the phrase 'be careful what you wish for'? Well, if you miss that wine cellar off your list... Now I reiterate, this is a future goal. It may be that you are fortunate enough to be at the stage to buy your forever home now but for most of you I want you to think bigger than your current needs/budget. Find as many images as you can to illustrate these points, or you can even draw it on yourself.

First home wish list

Now we are going to have to be realistic about the first step on the journey to this goal – the property you are about to buy. So do the same exercise we have just done for your dream home, but now more realistically for your first property. Ask yourself the following:

- What could I be flexible on?
- What could I go without?
- What will I absolutely refuse to go without?

When you pose each of these questions, really push yourself by asking 'why' to each of your answers (a bit like a really annoying toddler, don't let yourself off until you have exhausted all answers!).

Once that's done you should have a very realistic picture of the property you are looking to buy. There's a simple reason for doing this and I'd like you to try an experiment to illustrate my point. I want you to think of something small you might want to buy. It may be a jacket, a pair of shoes, a car even. What colour and style/make is it? Really picture it in your head. Suddenly you will notice that item all over the place. There's nothing spooky or spiritual about this, it's just the way the mind works. Once we focus on something, we can't help but notice it. It was always there, we just weren't tuned into it. Think Derren Brown! This is also why you have to be careful when you focus too much on the kind of property you *don't* want to have, as sure enough, it will keep popping up in your searches!

Where to buy

I would love to have a sea view, country pubs down the road, city nightlife within a cheap taxi ride home, great schools on my doorstep and be able to walk to work. Wouldn't that be nice eh? I find choosing 'where to buy' a fascinating subject. I have spoken to a lot of people who have complained about being shoehorned into a house not big enough for their burgeoning family. This is often the case for those desperate to stay inside the M25.

Remember my story, I was born in Australia, I grew up in Dorset, went to University in the Midlands, rented all over London and bought my first place in Folkestone, and now live in Sevenoaks, Kent. I guess that's why I don't feel the need to stick to one area. I'm also aware from my travels that whilst I lived in very central places in London like Camden, it wasn't an awful lot more convenient. I've just done a quick search and for the price I paid for my 7-bed house, I would get a 2-bed flat in Camden. I wouldn't even own it entirely as it would be leasehold. It would take me 35 minutes to get to work because it's not near a tube station. Where I live now takes 45 minutes door to door. So this is a very specific example but it shows that just because the flock want to live somewhere, it doesn't make it the most savvy location to buy in when it comes to climbing the property ladder.

You may desperately want to live in a particular location. It may be your number one priority, I get that. Where you live is really important. Remember though we have a plan here. If you can't afford to buy what you want where you want, we have to take another route. It may be that it's possible to buy fixer-uppers in your chosen area and gradually work your way towards your dream home. If that location is in great demand though you will probably have a huge amount of competition and will therefore need to stump up more cash. If you have the cash it's probably fine, but if not we need to look elsewhere, or work your way in, as I put it. If this just all feels like way too much hassle then this book is perhaps not for you and you have the following options:

- Choose to rent, because it's the only way you can afford to live in a big enough place in that area. This is definitely an option and if you have considered all others and this is still the most appealing then give up on the financial security of owning your own bricks and mortar and never look back. This is very common in a lot of European cultures after all.
- Buy a much smaller place than you require in your ideal location, but don't complain about it because that is the choice you made, location over size, so have no regrets.
- Win the lottery.
- Discover a long-lost, dying, rich relative…

I joke of course. You may find your career or business flourish and your means rapidly increase, but this is a book about climbing the property ladder in today's situation so forgive me!

Location fit for your exit plan

Whatever the route, we need to have our exit plan in mind, in case something happens and we can't pay the mortgage. If your exit plan is to have lodgers, or rent it out (remember with the latter you would be required to switch to a buy-to-let mortgage) then location *is* a consideration. Location is also important if you're planning to help pay for the mortgage with Airbnb guests. By that I don't mean it needs to be in the centre of your chosen city, or with seafront views. It's more about convenience. So think about who your potential lodger or renter is going to be. If it's a family home then schools are important. For the commuter, train stations are a must. Talk to agents to find out what renters are looking for in the area. It's important you have established the demand.

If you can be fairly flexible with your location, then finding an area with future developments in the pipeline will accelerate your journey up the ladder. Look out for areas with new transport links, new hospitals, or any kind of new community being built that will provide more employment opportunities, therefore attracting more people to the town in the coming years. The great thing about thinking like a property investor is that when you come to sell to move up the next rung of the ladder you will have a willing market of buyers as well.

Personal location needs

So this is just my way of getting you to think outside of the ideal town you're looking to live in...for now. I'm not saying this will be the case forever – keep that end goal in sight. If you are more tied to an area because of work hours or schools, then your ascent may be a little slower, but not impossible. In that case you want to look for roads that may be in the process of getting a facelift (a café opening up is always a good sign!). You will also need to be a bit cleverer with the property you choose, making sure you get it for a good price and with the potential for improving and/or increasing its size.

Some personal questions you may want to ask yourself when choosing a location are:

- Do I want to be able to walk to shops, a pub, train or bus station, work, school?
- Do I need a certain amount of greenery?
- Do I care what other properties on the road look like?
- Will I feel safe if walking back at night?
- Is traffic noise an issue for me?
- Is being able to walk around the corner for a pint of milk enough?

Write down which of these really matter to you and which you can live with or without.

Negative location factors

It's worth bearing in mind what can influence the value of an area. This helps you to assess it on your first visit, but you can also look into the future as to how your property will be affected by any changes. Here are some factors that have historically been detrimental to property prices:

- Poorly performing schools – check Ofsted results
- A Lidl (although I'm not sure that is still the case, judging by the amount of 4x4s in the car park of my local one!) – check local council planning
- High levels of crime – obviously – check crime map at www.police.uk
- Known flood plain – check environment agency flood map
- Electricity pylons or mobile masts – check with local council
- Trainers hung over the telephone wires (apparently drugs sold here!)
- Large constructions going up on your doorstep – unless these provide jobs (check local council planning)

If you're not familiar with an area, one of the best things you can do though is talk to the locals. Yes some of it will be hearsay, but you could glean some hidden gems or whopping warning signs you wouldn't necessarily find online. Don't underestimate your gut feeling as well. Just taking a day to do a drive around a few of your circled areas will give you a lot to go on. Whilst you may not be able to live in your dream location immediately, it's important you are happy with where you are based for the time being.

If you do choose a location far away from where you live now, I would really advise you rent there for a few months, before taking the plunge. It will make house-hunting much easier, but will also help you to decide if this is the best place for you to buy right now. If it's further from work don't forget to add the extra travel costs to your outgoings calculations as well – although it's worth having that conversation with work, about flexible hours, so you're not paying peak prices.

Type of property – new build or old wreck?

'Everybody loves a fixer-upper' as the song goes...from *Frozen*... sorry too much Disney in my life. In my experience, it's not exactly true. I've never once got into a bidding war on the shabby places I've bought. This is partly because I would walk away if I couldn't get a property for a good price. It also seems to be that more people want a property that at worst needs a lick of paint. Even better if it's ready for them to move in and relax, complete with a top of the range fridge!

I like to buy a place that has a really grotty fridge, which perches precariously in a cold lean-to...preferably with rotting food in it! That's why I don't pay the asking price for the houses I choose. I then do them up and sell them to lovers of finished, shiny houses!

Fixer-upper
There are many pitfalls to buying old, like the fact the property is...well...old! Houses built pre central heating often struggle with modern day needs. Unless the previous owners have been fastidious, there is likely to be some kind of problem with

crumbling walls, out-dated plumbing and electrics, single glazed windows, damp issues, unfit roofs. This is why it is worth getting a full survey done and taking a builder along, so you know what you are letting yourself in for. If it's a real dump and doesn't have certain aspects, like a plumbed-in kitchen, you can even have difficulty getting a mortgage.

But I love a fixer-upper. Nothing gets me more excited than arriving at a house oozing nicotine, with an ill-fitting front door! If you are buying to do somewhere up, obviously the cost will vary massively depending on any issues, area and the age of the property. If you are a lover of recently refurbished properties it's likely that you are buying from an investor who has done a quick turnaround finish on a tired place and made a nice tidy profit at your expense.

The only thing to be aware of is that at the lower end of the market you may find there's more interest from investors. If this is your first property though, remember you are chain free and will be paying less to no stamp duty so are in a much more desirable position. As you move up the ladder, the competition decreases. This is partly because the capital value versus rental value becomes greater and therefore more risky and less appealing for the bulk of investors. But also because for domestic buyers, the bigger the house, the more kids are likely to be involved, leading to a need for stability and less time to spend on renovating.

The inbetweener
The inbetweener is the kind of place that is 'fine'. This means it could do with a lick of paint, but would be OK to move into straight away. You would maybe even move in and find you don't notice the marks on the walls. You may get lucky with this kind of property, but there are often hidden issues and you will probably still pay at least market price for it, which makes it harder to climb the ladder.

New-builds
Then there are new-builds. There is something very appealing about a new-build home. Everything is...well...new! I've filmed at a lot of high quality new-build developments, and they do feel very shiny and modern (obviously). They usually exercise a very clever use of space and often have a wonderful community feel

to them because of the manicured communal areas. A new-build should be more energy efficient as a result as well. Most come with an NHBC 10 year warranty and many builders give two year guarantees as well.

Of course there are an increasing amount of them as the government pledges to build more to ease the housing crisis. In theory this should bring the price of them down, but that doesn't always seem to correlate. As I mentioned earlier, as a first-time buyer you may be able to benefit from the Starter Homes Scheme if you go for a new-build. It may help you get on the ladder, but remember we are looking to climb the ladder so we need future proofing in our decision-making. The mortgage process for a newbie can also be a bit more problematic as providers tend to put a cap on the percentage they will offer, meaning you need more cash. With new-builds you quite often have service charges, which you need to factor into your bills.

There is a massive difference between a high-end and lower market developer. If your budget is tight it is likely you will be looking at the latter. You can usually kiss goodbye to any potential to expand. Don't expect 'new' stuff to stay new as well. There are often teething problems – other than just cracks in walls, which are inevitable settling issues. I've heard of some lower-end developers who want to just get them up as quickly as possible and then deal (or not deal) with any issues retrospectively. Plumbing and drainage can be one of the problems you come across, because until you move in, the property hasn't been tried and tested. Whilst the high-end developers seem to be quick to rectify most issues, I have heard some shocking stories at the lower end where the onus is on the new owner to prove that problems are down to the builders. Of course this isn't going to be the case with all developers and with all new-builds, but it's important that you understand 'new' doesn't necessarily mean 'problem free'.

If life is just too stressful, and you just want to be able to move in and unpack then a new-build by a reputable developer is probably your cup of tea, and should increase in value over time, but it's not what this book is about.

Self-build

I think it's worth covering this, although one of the issues with self-builds is you need more cash and it certainly helps to have experience. The benefits are that you can build VAT free, to a degree you can have influence over the design, and control over the quality of the build. It should be more energy efficient and it should cost you less overall than buying a pre-existing property. But you do need to find the land (becoming increasingly difficult) and you are likely to come up against people with more funds and experience when you do find the plot. You then need to be able to get planning permission for that land (unless it comes with it). If you don't have the cash, you need a different type of mortgage to do a self-build, but you can switch once it's built.

To do list

- Create your 'forever home' vision board
- Write a realistic wish list for your first property
- Eliminate anything from that list you could live without
- Decide what you can and can't live without when it comes to a location
- Consider a few locations you could move out to
- Check out property prices in these areas
- Speak to local agents to find out rental demand (in case you need to depend on your exit plan in the future)
- Research plans for the area using the local council website and other online resources
- Eliminate inappropriate areas
- Visit the locations in your final shortlist
- Speak to local residents
- Decide how much of a project you want to go for (if at all)

CHAPTER 5:
How to find a property

How to find a property

You may think this is the easy bit as you've been searching Rightmove and Zoopla since well before you got a deposit together. You can't help but stop when you pass by an estate agent's window. That's what everyone else does right? Indeed most people do and that's why we need to take a different approach. Yes the Internet is going to be part of your strategy, but not the whole of it.

Internet search portals

There are a number of these and they are very useful. It's a good idea to include some of the lesser known ones as well. Although it's likely that you will find most of the market on Rightmove, Zoopla and Prime Location there may be a few stragglers elsewhere. This has become more the case since folk are coming around to the idea of selling without traditional agents.

Here are just a few to look at, but do your own internet search as well, as sites will be popping up all the time. Don't just go with the first page as the worse the SEO of that site is the more likely you will find something that others won't!

- Rightmove.co.uk
- Zoopla.co.uk
- PrimeLocation.com
- OnTheMarket.com
- Houseladder.co.uk
- Home.co.uk

One thing to be wary of is that although the 'guestimates' that some of these sites provide are helpful to gauge the market value of a certain type of property in an area, they are not to be taken too literally for an individual property. If something has been done up, or indeed fallen into disrepair, they can only know this if the owner goes in and updates it. To that point, there's nothing to stop the vendor from inflating the price of their property as well!

If the homes that have caught your fancy on these sites are with a high street agent, I would advise you go directly to them. I have found that the 'contact the agent' button often doesn't seem to get me anywhere. I'm not sure if this is because they go to an email list that simply isn't checked enough, or that they get inundated with requests for details via the search engines, so they can't possibly take them all seriously. One thing I do know is that there are times when the market moves very quickly so there's no time to wait for call-backs.

Agents

Of course there's one sure-fire way to have access to the majority of available 'stock', as they put it. That's right, to a lot of agents your future home is just stock and that is something to bear in mind when you are approaching them.

You might visit the high street of your chosen area and do it that way around. But don't forget that small, independent agents still exist and may be in more obscure positions away from the main area, so you don't want to miss these. I actually think the best thing you can do is make a list of the agents that tend to deal with the size and type of property you are after. You can glean this information from a combination of looking at search engines and visiting their sites, which you might find by hunting online. Remember the smaller independent ones will often have properties that were listed with them because the vendor likes to be loyal to local businesses. They may have used them before or been recommended by a friend. They do not appear as high up on the search engines, because they don't have the same budget as the national firms. So there is less competition from other buyers who don't bother to scroll down further than the first page in their search. They may also have fewer properties so you get a more personal service.

Now that you have your list, you want to meet them. Yep, I know that may seem like a faff, but it's worth it, trust me. Once you have a relationship with them you will also then know where to go when you want to sell yours and move up the ladder. The best idea is to book appointments to see specific agents in the area, then you know you can cram as many into your day as possible. If they have some properties you want to look at then it's worth booking the viewings on the same day, but that all depends on your available time and how close you are currently to the location.

Something to always keep at the forefront of your mind is that estate agents earn most of their living by commission. The vendor is their client. This doesn't always tally for those who want the quickest sale possible. I have met some master actors as well who are just incredible at making you think they are on your side!!!! You *do* want to strike up a relationship with them though. This is partly because you want to be at the forefront of their minds when any new houses come on the market. But also because isn't life just more enjoyable when we make friends?!

If you are a first-time buyer, you want them to get excited about this fact as the lack of chain trailing behind you makes you desirable. If you're a cash buyer, lucky thing, even better. Impress upon them that if you find something you like you will act quickly on it. Agents love buyers like that. They don't like ditherers! Don't forget that if you're looking for a doer-upper then you will have competition from investors who will have made it their business to be the first in line when something comes along.

One thing to be aware of is that they will often aim to upsell. By that, I mean they know the emotional value of 'the right place'. They know that when you're saying you can afford £150k you really mean that if it were 'the right place' you would find the means to stretch to £175k if it was the difference between getting it and missing out. I don't want to sound too negative about agents, as I have worked with some very honest, diligent ones. My stepbrother is one of the good eggs in fact! But there are some that, particularly in bad markets, can't help themselves as they are so reliant on the commission to earn a living.

Online agents

You are less likely to be able to build a relationship when a house is on with an online agent. It may be that apart from the viewing bookings you will be dealing directly with the vendor. Don't assume you will just come across their properties on the search portals. It may be due to some kind of error one doesn't pop up in your investigation so it's worth looking directly at the online agency sites, in case any have slipped through the net.

Local paper

It may seem ultra old-school to look at a local newspaper, but people do still use them to sell a house. Imagine the scenario; an elderly couple are downsizing. They have never liked using estate agents, but also don't use the Internet, so the first thing they are going to do is reach for the local paper as that's how it was done in the old days. These will be rare occasions but they can be gems when you find them.

Auction

Property auctions can be fantastic places to pick up doer-uppers, but you will invariably be up against experienced investors. Don't let that put you off though! Buying at auction, however, is not something to do on a whim. Your first time bidding at auction is likely to be a scary, but thrilling experience, so here are some pointers.

As you step through the door of the auction house to buy for the first time, you should have already practised by attending at least one other auction. It's paramount that when you actually come to buy, you're feeling reasonably confident, level-headed and very much prepared. So on your first day it's worth even picking a property to bid on in your head. Just sit on your hands though in case you get carried away!

The auction house will release a catalogue of all the lots about a month beforehand. This means you have plenty of time to view any relevant properties. Do this thoroughly and don't just assume you're getting a bargain because it's at auction. Believe it or not there are wholesalers that will scuff up a property so that inexperienced buyers will think they are getting a great deal, when actually they've elevated the price! Crazy I know, but I've heard some stories! The auctioneers will also have a legal pack which you can usually get online. You and your solicitor should go through this before the auction.

Buying at auction is faster than other routes, but this means you need to be prepared. You must come with money and identification. You also need to have the funds available. This includes a 10% deposit ready on the day of the auction, as the contracts will be signed there and then. The other 90% will be payable within 28 days usually, although this can vary between lots. If you need a mortgage, have this arranged in principle before auction day.

It may be a long day, and not always in the most comfortable room, so come prepared. You will be grateful for layered clothing and a packed lunch so you don't have to leave. You want to be in your best state as an auction athlete!

Position is everything. It's best to stand at the sides or back when bidding so you can have a clear view of the room and your competitors! It can help to know the lingo too. The 'guide price' is what the property is expected to sell for and what the vendor is hoping to achieve. The 'reserve price', however, is what must be reached for the auction to be valid. You can still make an offer afterwards if the property doesn't reach the reserve and is withdrawn. The reserve price is confidential, but you might start by pitching it close to the amount at which it was withdrawn.

When bidding, be aware that the auctioneer is allowed to 'bid-off-the-wall', which is essentially pretending someone else is bidding against you. This is only allowed up to the reserve price – so don't get stroppy if you think he's being naughty, as you wouldn't have got it below the reserve anyway! The auctioneer can also take proxy bids. This would be prearranged between the auctioneer and a bidder who can't attend, as opposed to those in the room, or on the phone.

Remember when the gavel comes down, if you were the last bidder you are legally bound to buy the property, warts and all!

Repossession properties

There are some agents that specialise in repossessed property. A quick search online will find these. You can often tell when the property is being sold under these circumstances from the pictures as there is usually tape across toilets and appliances. You may get a bargain with these as the current owner (often a bank) is merely looking to recoup costs as quickly as possible. You will probably have lots of competition from investors though.

Property scouts

If you're adamant you want a doer-upper, it might make sense for you to register with some property scouts. These are people who find properties with potential for investors. There's nothing to say they wouldn't work with you. They charge a commission if you buy the home they introduce you to though, so if money is tight this may be a time-saver but a luxury you can't afford. Also if you do go with one, you want to make sure you do all your own due diligence as well, no matter how thorough they seem to be.

Proactive house-hunting

How about being more proactive even? Placing an ad yourself in the local paper detailing the kind of property you're after could motivate someone who hasn't pulled their finger out as yet, but is really keen to sell. The same goes for local online publications as well, although usually these days they are one of a kind.

Who have we established is often looking to move up the property ladder? Parents of course. Mums and dads often have an amazing network. They also like to gossip. If you know an area you're keen on buying in, posting on the local mums or dads online groups could be a very quick way of finding people who love the idea of a very simple transaction with a keen buyer.

Leafleting!

Whaaaat? I hear you say! I'm sharing a little property investor's trick with you here. If you find a particular road you're interested in, what's the harm in making up a leaflet to put through people's doors? This is something I've advised people that have missed out on a house in the ideal street to do as well. I've even knocked on the door when I've seen a house that needs some TLC. I just ask them if they have thought of selling and that I could handle everything to make their lives easier. This is all true of course, but sometimes if people don't have the motivation to move that's all they need – if they don't have to pay agents' fees that's just a bonus for them.

Empty houses

When you're out and about keep an eye open for properties that look like they are empty. Local authorities are keen to have these filled and will often have an empty property officer who may be able to link you up with the owner. If it has fallen into disrepair it's worth asking if there are any grants on offer. Make sure you get the property looked over by a builder and a surveyor though as if it's been vacant for a long time it may be more expensive than you think to fix.

To do list

- Register with all search portals so you are getting notifications
- Start a spread sheet or some record of properties of interest
- Research agents in the areas you are looking at
- Book to meet agents relevant to the level of property you are looking at
- Keep a note of their names and anything you learned about them
- Check out the local paper for anybody selling
- Register with auction houses so you are receiving alerts
- Rehearse at an auction
- Contact local property scouts
- Put out the feelers among local online forums
- Put together a leaflet to distribute in your ideal roads
- Look out for empty properties and contact the council for help

CHAPTER 6:
Bagging a bargain

Who is the ideal vendor?

This is going to sound heartless but where property is concerned you are always likely to do best when someone else is down on their luck. This is very different to scamming someone or taking advantage of them, it's just that their priority is going to be different to yours. Their current situation means they are not focussing on climbing the property ladder. Remember that a property is only worth what someone is prepared to pay for it and most of the flats and houses I've bought, nobody else wanted, but the vendor really needed to sell. People often refer to the three Ds – divorce, death and debt, and as uncomfortable as it feels, these are the situations where the vendor will not be holding out for an inflated price.

Divorce
When a couple sadly decide to divorce, they usually haven't come to that decision easily. So by the time it happens, they want it to be quick and clean, like ripping off a plaster. Obviously this isn't always the case as it may be a one-sided split. I have had to deal with this before when the wife couldn't sell quickly enough, no matter what she got, whilst the reluctant husband was dragging his heels. They were actually both still living in the house, but the agent had to speak to each of them individually to get answers to EVERY one of my questions! Suffice to say, this was a painful example, and it also saddened me greatly, but at the end of the day they needed to sell.

Debt
If debt is the reason someone is selling, they need to sell quickly. If you're chain free, you are a more tempting buyer and because they are in a hurry they are not about to hold out for the best possible price. Time is ticking by before they lose the house to the mortgage provider. Once that has happened the bank is also not bothered about sticking around for the best price because they just want the

cash. There are some agencies whose main stock is under the latter conditions. They tend to have a whole host of investors on their books looking to buy quickly, but that's not to say you can't get in there as well – you just need to make sure you have also established a good relationship.

Death

Would you feel funny about buying a house that someone died in? If so you're not alone, but you do need to get over it. Death is something that comes to us all (in case you didn't know!). When a house is being sold because someone has died, it is just part of the circle of life, imitated in property. I have known some buyers who won't even look at a property because the previous owner had died (and not even necessarily in the house!). This means there may be less competition. If we are to assume that person was old and frail, it's likely the property has fallen into disrepair and hasn't been decorated in quite a while, so will be the perfect doer-upper. In most cases it's been inherited by their children, who are grateful just for the cash, it's not like they need the top value in order to move up the ladder as it's a sudden injection of money. Although that's not always the case! If there is inheritance tax to pay, they may be in a hurry to sell sometimes too. If an elderly parent has had to move into a home you will often find the offspring need to sell quickly as they have to pay for the extortionate nursing costs as well.

Urgent sellers

Being in a hurry makes someone the ideal person to buy from. Often if a vendor has found their perfect property they have more of an incentive to accept a lower offer. If they have set their hearts on it and desperately don't want to miss out they will be keen to get rid of theirs as quickly as possible. Of course this doesn't always correlate, as they will need to fetch a certain amount to be able to afford said property.

Left on the shelf

A property that has been on the market for a while with no movement, either has something wrong with it or it has been priced incorrectly. The vendor will need to drop their price if they are serious about selling, and by now they are often totally fed up with the whole process – particularly if they have had offers that have fallen through. Cleaning/tidying your house for endless viewings is pretty soul-destroying after all. Now you may not glean this information until you have spoken with the agent, and even then you can expect some to be held back. A trick that some vendors/ agents do is they take a property off the market and down from all the online sites before dropping the price and relaunching it so new buyers to the market think it is fresh and a potential hot potato. This is why it's worth keeping an eye on what's out there from day one. It is maybe a question to ask the vendor (or a neighbour!) 'wasn't this on the market a few months ago?'.

When you start house-hunting make a note of suitable properties that are 'under offer' even. If they come back on the market, and they often do, the vendor may be in even more of a hurry as they are already that far down the line with the home they are hoping to buy. If you are a chain free buyer you would be the ideal person to help them get to the finish line.

Property with potential

You won't necessarily know the situation of the seller by merely looking online of course. What you need is the following list of criteria to spot a property with potential:
- ✓ Freehold
- ✓ In need of modernisation
- ✓ Possibility to expand
- ✓ Good current location
- ✓ A location that is going up in the world
- ✓ A suitable rental property if everything goes belly up
- ✓ Something quirky

Freehold v. leasehold

If you can only afford a flat, it is likely to be leasehold. Leasehold means that you just have a lease from the freeholder to use the home for the duration of the lease. You usually have to pay an annual ground rent and when the lease expires the freeholder will take back ownership of the property. But you should be able to pay to extend the lease. There will generally be a management company looking after any maintenance of the property and grounds, the cost of which is usually covered by the leaseholders. You also would need to get permission from the freeholder for any extensive improvements you want to make.

Here follows the story of my first and final experience of being a leaseholder. It was a basement flat in an Edwardian building that was about four storeys high, from what I remember. We were expected to pay the maintenance company for things like cleaning the communal internal areas and tending the garden. Our flat didn't even have access to the internal areas as we had a separate entrance and the garden wasn't touched the whole time we lived there! The last straw was when we were asked to pay thousands of pounds towards the cost of fixing the roof. I vowed to never go leasehold again!

It may be that you have no choice because of your budget. Buying somewhere with a short lease, if you can afford to increase that lease, can be a way to increase the value of the property – so long as you get it for a really good price *because* of the short lease! You may also be able to club together with the other leaseholders to buy the freehold of the property, but there's no guarantee when you buy that you will be able to do this, or that your new neighbours will have the desire or cash to do so with you.

If you are following my plan it is better to go freehold, but then my first place was leasehold and I still made money on it so I will leave that to your judgement!

In need of modernisation

'In need of modernisation' is diplomatic estate agent's speak for 'my client's place is a &*%$ hole'! Well actually it can mean anything from the property just needing new carpets, refreshed walls, and new kitchen and bathroom furniture, to 'somebody was found buried in the wall cavities' (or at least that's what it smells like when you go round to view it!).

If a property doesn't need a lick of paint at the very least, it is unlikely it will help you move up the ladder quickly. Don't be fooled by estate agents' photos though as they are the masters of getting feet through the door. You can usually assume that if pictures of certain rooms have been omitted they are in a bad state! 'In need of modernisation' is my number one priority when looking for a property.

Possibility to expand

This is always an exciting prospect and if you can add space it's usually the best way to add value to a property, so long as there is the demand in the area.

If there's no roof conversion check out the rest of the road to see if anyone else has dormers. If they have then they've set a precedent and it should be easier to get planning permission, if that's even necessary. How much space is there out the back? Could we maybe extend out and/or upwards? Bungalows are great for these kinds of projects as they usually sit on a considerable amount of land. They can tend to be like hen's teeth when they go up for sale though for that very reason. Why not leaflet a bungalow heavy area and get in first! One thing to consider is that planning permission to extend out the front is often harder to gain. If it is a corner plot, with two entrances, there can sometimes be ambiguity as to which side is considered to be the front.

If there's a basement that's not being used at the moment, this is also extra space you could make liveable to increase the amount of rooms. Bear in mind though that if there is a damp issue it can be costly to correct and make watertight. In squeezed London, it's quite common these days to extend downwards to make underground space. Apparently this can even be beneficial if there is a subsidence issue as you will be underpinning and therefore strengthening. It is pretty costly though.

Rather than adding space, you might be able to chop up over-sized rooms to increase the amount of bedrooms it has. This has to be done sympathetically though so that the property isn't adversely affected in other ways. Turning a dining room into a bedroom may work for the rental market but not when it comes to someone's home. It also doesn't make much difference in areas like London as people judge a property more by its square footage than the amount of rooms it has.

With all these conceivable space makers, bear in mind that you don't need the available cash right now at the time of buying. It is worth looking at the potential, how much that would cost and the value it's likely to add to the property. You also need to think about demand. A house is only worth what people are prepared to pay for it and there tends to be a ceiling in an area. If you overdevelop a property, but in doing so reduce the footfall when it comes to selling, you may end up out of pocket.

Good current location

Remember our exit plan? I know I said that you won't necessarily be going for your dream location straight away, but if you go for somewhere in the back of beyond, far from transport links, with failing schools, high crime rates and high unemployment rates, you may pick it up for a song, but you may also struggle to sell later. It probably won't be worth making any improvements because the demand is coming from people who can't afford the luxury of a newly fitted kitchen, bathroom and carpet. If you end up needing to rent it out you may also struggle, or at least you're likely to have longer void periods – meanwhile you're still having to pay the mortgage.

A location with potential

This is actually an even better option. It takes a bit of research but finding areas that are going up in the world are real winners. There may be new transport links connecting once isolated communities to city centres. If new job opportunities are being introduced to the area with large businesses or services being opened up, the demand increases. Remember the more people want something, the higher its value. It could be something as simple as a school becoming an academy or having investment pumped into it. These will all affect the local market. Even a Waitrose opening up nearby can benefit the asset value of its neighbours. It's usually a strong indicator that their research has told them it's a good place to open a shop as well don't forget.

More locally, if you see a road that maybe looks a little rough, but there are a few houses that have recently been refurbished, and sold or rented easily, it's worth investigating. The improvement can have a snowball effect, but you might need to hang on in there a bit longer to see the benefits.

Suitable rental property

We are back to that exit plan again. Remember if all goes belly up, you want to be able to hold onto the property if possible. In order to even get on the property ladder it may be you're going to need to have a lodger or Airbnb a room, or even the whole property during a time you strategically arrange to 'catch up' with friends and family!

You can quite easily work out how much you would fetch with some quick Internet research into who would be your competition. It's back to your online search engines to check out the rental value for similar properties in the road. Talking to a rental agent is also really worthwhile as they will be able to guide you on demand and rental value. Remember to allow for tax when necessary.

Something quirky

This is an odd one, but sometimes there may be something quite small, and frankly daft, that is putting off other buyers. If *you* can look past this it will go in your favour of course. For example, those who are superstitious may not touch a house numbered 13, which may mean you get it for below market price. You can then replace the number with a house name. Always look for the solution though, because if you can't find one you will simply have the same problem when selling the home yourself.

CHAPTER 7:
Savvy house hunting

Viewings spread sheet – yes really!

Am I going to lose you here? OK so you don't necessarily need to put together a spreadsheet, although if you're like my husband Andy, who can't get enough of them, go for it! What you don't want though, are scraps of paper here and there, scattered notes on your phone, or even worse in your head! We need to be organised, as it may be the biggest investment we ever make in our lifetime.

If you're a bit more old school and want to write things down, get yourself a notebook to dedicate to the cause so everything is in one place.

Being organised like this means you can arrange your viewings easily, make your notes once you've viewed the property, and keep an eye on how prices are moving if you end up looking for a while. You would be amazed at how phased you can get after even just a day of viewing properties. It can get very confusing – thinking a lounge you liked was at one property when that was the one that didn't have any windows, but did have off-street parking!

Booking your viewings

Viewing properties can sometimes feel like a military operation! I've always been quite surprised by how difficult it can be to book to view a house or flat. I've come across agents not calling me back – although this doesn't happen if you've built the right relationship remember. I've come across vendors being difficult about evening viewings. I've come across agents not being prepared to do a viewing after 6pm. I've come across vendors not being contactable to get the keys. I've wanted to scream from the rooftops PEOPLE I WANT TO VIEW YOUR RUDDY HOME AS I MAY WANT TO BUY IT!

The reason I am telling this is that from start to finish the whole buying/selling of a property can be incredibly frustrating. The more you do it, the more you become numb to the frustrations. It doesn't hurt as much when you know what to expect, so I want you to be able to laugh it off when you come across these situations, and simply say 'oh yeah Georgina said this would happen'. I want this for you because life is too short, and stressful enough as it is, but I also want you as level-headed in this process as possible as we are going to buy with our brains first. The heart is only a secondary concern. Remember if they are being difficult about arranging the viewing, it will be the same for everyone, which will probably have put others off – last man standing and all that!

Rate the properties you find out of 10 so you have your prioritised list. You want to make sure you're seeing the ones you're really keen on first. I like viewing as many as possible in a day, so I can do a like-for-like comparison. In my opinion it's worth taking a day or two off work to do this. Remember to keep a note of the address, the agents and the agent's mobile number in case you are delayed at all. Ask about where you can park too. If you're seeing a few in a day you need it to be a slick operation. If the properties are close to each other I usually allow for between 30 and 45 minutes for the viewing and to get to the next one. Again having this schedule written down, will really help you concentrate on the matter in hand. Either ask the agent to post or email the particulars so you can print them out and study in advance.

Property viewing checklist

Having moved 28 times, viewed many potential investment properties, and helped others to buy theirs, it goes without saying I have poked my nose around a fair few places in my life. The following list has been many years in the making, starting from as far back as when I was four years old (my first memory of viewing a house!), so I thought it might be worth sharing this with you. It's also a good idea to jump ahead to the 'how to make improvements' section of this book before viewing properties so you can start to think about how you might make it work for you if you were to buy it.

Know your particulars inside out

Really study the details sent by the agent. But be warned that the photos may not be true to life – expect to be a little disappointed! Remember they are all about getting bums on seats. The more people that come through the door, the more likely it will sell as it can be a numbers game sometimes. Also they can say they have done their job and that it's the house's fault – or at least it's time to drop the price, which means a quicker sale!

Note what is missing from the particulars. If there are certain rooms not included, it usually means they would put people off if shown! I actually get quite excited when this happens as I know it means it will whittle down the competition and may be more of a doer-upper than is suggested. If you have studied the particulars you are more likely to notice the important points *not* included. Oh and don't take them at face value – I once viewed a house that apparently came with a garage. It transpired, during the actual sale, that the vendor was merely renting and there was no guarantee I'd be able to rent it myself if I bought the house! To be fair I think the vendor had hoodwinked the agent, but it's a lesson to not believe everything you read.

Come armed with questions and don't let the agent shy away from answering them. Sometimes you may be shown around by a 'viewing assistant'. This is most common during the evenings and weekends. You can certainly ask them your questions, but it's worth double-checking with the actual agent as they should be more knowledgeable. In one instance I had to show the viewing assistant where the property's garage was as it wasn't attached to the house – I'd clearly done my homework better than her!

Do a drive-by

If it's a property you are really keen on, your appointment shouldn't be the first time you view it. You would be amazed at the preparation people go to for viewings. I once turned up early (something else I like to do – annoying right?!), the vendor was actually sticky-tacking the front gate post to stay upright as it had come away from the fence. If this was her quick fix outside who knows what was going on inside!

People have been known to actually pay neighbours to park away if their cars aren't impressive enough – imagine that conversation!!! Have a little drive by at different times of the day. Get out and walk around. Definitely talk to neighbours. It's a legal requirement to give details of a neighbour dispute, but some may slip through the net. You are more likely to get an honest picture of the road from Doris who lives opposite.

If the main selling point is the location, test out the time it takes to get to the station or the local school. Do this at different times of the day so you can get a true feel for the area – is it always quiet? If it's near a school is it like Piccadilly Circus at pick up time? These are important factors that might not be apparent at just a single viewing.

Poker face

This is one my parents taught me as a child. Never show excitement to either the vendor or the agent! You don't want to be too negative though either. Let's face it, someone's home is very personal to them and it's cruel to crush their soul by pointing out orange pine cladding went out of fashion in the 70s, and unlike other fashions hasn't come back around again! Also you are likely to create a hostile relationship – not great for negotiation. You would be amazed at how much a vendor can dig their heels in if they decide they don't want their family home to be lived in by a tactless so and so!

These days, particularly with the rise of online agents, it's more common than it used to be for the vendor to show you around the house and if there's a chance to meet them it's always a good thing. Ask directly why are they selling? If you know the answer to that it can help you to understand their situation. If they're in a hurry you might get away with a cheeky offer, if not you will have to come to terms with the fact they may hold out for a higher price.

Be a surveyor

By this I don't mean it negates the need to use a properly qualified surveyor as the sale progresses! There are certain things you want to look out for from the start as these issues should affect how much you offer.

Damp

Damp is a really important thing to check for. There's good and bad damp though. Well actually there's bad, and very bad damp, it's never good! For example, I've had a place where the smell hit you when you entered the front door. It turned out to be due to a hole in the porch roof directing rainwater to an internal wall. That was relatively easy to fix. This is classed as penetrating damp, which can also be down to cracks in walls and roof issues.

You could go as far as to buy, borrow or rent a damp meter. Look out for hotspots (or soggy spots as they should be known!) like chimneybreasts – particularly if there is a loft conversion. These things can sometimes be down to ageing lead flashing around the chimney. Or if the chimney isn't in use anymore but is still open to the elements it collects water – so a simple solution is to put a cap on the chimney pot. If a fireplace has been blocked up, a vent will prevent damp at the bottom.

Rising damp is another issue though and one that is likely to be costly, if not impossible to fix. There are also things like dry rot and wet rot that you may not be able to uncover as they are below floorboards. Look out for bouncy floorboards, salt deposits and flaky paint at low levels on the ground floor. It could be a minor issue though like flowerbeds above the damp course or broken guttering or downpipes.

Condensation is one of the most common issues. Older houses weren't built with modern living, such as radiators, in mind. There's usually not enough ventilation and this is when condensation occurs.

If you buy the property with damp issues you would get an expert in to fix them, but for now it's enough to recognise the warning signs. Look out for mould, flaking plaster, bubbling wallpaper and watermarks on walls and ceilings. It's not necessarily a reason not to buy, but should be a big consideration when negotiating.

Is it a crack den?

Hairline cracks are to be expected, but major cracks can be a sign of subsidence. If you spot the latter you must get a structural survey done. Cracks will appear even in new buildings, and certainly in old ones – my Victorian house is riddled with them! You will often see them coming from door and window frames and they are usually due to settlement in new builds or where walls have been newly plastered in refurbished older buildings. The time you want to worry is when they are over 15mm, but even then there are solutions, they are just likely to be costly so should affect the price you pay. If you are going ahead with the sale on a property with major cracks, it would also be prudent to get an expert in so you aren't just guestimating the expense you may incur.

Also look out for vegetation around the building. If you use the height of a tree as a guide, imagine its roots could be three times as long and sucking out water from the ground. Be particularly wary of trees like Leylandii, which are notoriously bad news for houses. Anything closer than 20 feet is a potential problem. Sometimes cutting them down causes drainage problems as the tree is no longer sucking the water out of the soil, so this can be a costly problem to rectify.

Does it suit *your* needs?
By this I mean, think about the furniture you have, the rooms you tend to spend most of your time in. Is there enough storage? OK so this may not be your forever home, but you do need to live fairly comfortably there for a short while.

Will it fit the life-size Dr Who cardboard cut-out you keep in your kitchen…just as an example?! We struggled to find a house with a master bedroom to fit our super king size four-poster bed. Sloping ceilings in bedrooms, may add character but also force you to keep wardrobes elsewhere, which can be a pain. It's also not the end of the world and if it has massive potential and ticks a lot of other boxes then having a clear-out might be a better option (it often is). Maybe the time-lord has had his day…for example!

Do the stamp and knock
If you're looking to improve a property, sometimes opening it up can modernise and make it seem larger and lighter. It's also desirable for the bulk of today's homebuyers to have an open-plan style. A really easy and cost effective way of doing this is by simply knocking down stud walls, usually added by previous generations.

Tapping the wall to hear if there's a hollow sound will tell you if the wall is weight bearing or not.

I also go around stamping my feet – not so that I can get my own way (although that does happen) but so I can work out if there might be some original floorboards under the carpet, which could save me money.

New kitchen needed?

If the kitchen looks like it needs to be replaced because it's shabby or out-dated, check inside the cupboards as you may find that if the layout and the carcasses are good, you only need to replace or paint the doors and get a new worktop.

See through the smoke and mirrors

I will be going through every trick in the book with you later when it comes to selling. It's not about deceiving potential buyers, more about displaying what you have to offer in the best light. When you're buying though you need to be able to see through certain techniques that may be creating a red herring to divert your eye from something they don't want you to notice.

Mirrors are awesome. I love them and have way too many in my home! They can give extra light and make a room seem a lot more spacious. If it comes down to comparing that feeling of space with another property, make a note of any strategically placed mirrors, and look at what the *actual* measurements are telling you.

Watch out for clever use of lighting as well. Light can also make a room feel bigger or smaller. If a place feels dingy because they haven't been clever about the lighting it can be an easy fix, so worth bearing in mind if that's putting you off an otherwise desirable property. Talking of light you need to know which direction the property faces as well so you understand when, if at all, it will have sunlight. Daylight can have a big impact on the appeal of a property. If it's going to be dark most of the day it will be harder to sell. People will pay a premium for south facing gardens. The particulars will often tell you the direction, but double-check it. I have a compass app on my phone I whip out!

We all know the old trick of using smells like coffee brewing and bread baking to lead your senses astray. If there are scented candles burning everywhere though, try and smell through it! Are they attempting to mask the scent of eau de dog, cigarettes or damp?!

The roof

Have as close a look at the roof as you can. This can be a very expensive thing to correct. Whether it's a tiled or a flat roof it will have a shelf life, so you need to be aware if that is a consideration. Sometimes a roof has been retiled with cement ones which used to be fashionable. These are incredibly heavy and can actually cause sagging, so watch out for them. Ask to go up into the loft so you can get a proper look, if they are reluctant to let you, it's worth insisting during a second viewing. When checking the loft, do so without the light on so you can see if there is any daylight leaking through the roof. Also look out for any insulation in the roof – this could be an easy improvement for you to make.

Windows

If the property doesn't have double-glazing it could cost a fortune to heat. Also if it's not double-glazed the frames could very well be old and potentially rotting as well. Even if it is double-glazed, how good are the windows, and do they come with the appropriate certificates? I've seen some really bad UPVC windows. If you just trust that the place is double-glazed you may have an expensive shock coming when you have to replace them anyway. If the frames are yellowing, it's a bad sign. This should all come out during the sale, but if you can find out earlier on it can help your decision when making an offer. If you have to replace these it could be your single biggest cost of the renovation.

Electrics and plumbing

How old are the sockets? Ask to see the fuse box – if that's old it's an indication you may well need to have the whole place rewired, which again will cost you a pretty penny. The same goes for the plumbing situation. Trust your instincts. If it feels wrong, it most likely is. Try running taps and showers to see the pressure. Generally clunking noises are not a good sign! Also, ask to see the boiler. Although even if it is new it still needs to be appropriate for the property. I had to replace a two-year-old boiler once on a property I'd just bought. One of the selling points was the 'relatively new boiler', but it turned out it wasn't big enough for the house! If there is no central heating, this is a way to add value alone as many people wouldn't touch it with a barge pole in its current state.

It's also good to know how much a place costs to run. I am just pretty forthright and ask to see a few bills as it would just be human nature for someone to be economical with the truth on this one! Firstly, I want to know I'm not going to be living in an ice-box, as I'm a bit of a reptile. Secondly, I'm not a fan of throwing away both money and the earth's resources!

Get a builder's opinion

These days I wouldn't consider buying a place until my friend 'Doug the builder' had been to see it. His decades of experience in dealing with problem properties means he's seen it all, knows the warning signs and how much any problems are likely to cost to fix. He's always going to spot something I've missed. It's worth finding a builder you feel you can trust to do this. They will often give you half an hour of their time for free as there is potential work for them in the near future. Even a small fee is worth paying if it helps you to understand the cost of doing up the property before you make your offer.

Parking

Even if you don't own a car, you need to be on top of the parking situation as this may be an issue to someone else when you go on to sell. If it's on-street parking how close will you be able to get to your front door on a regular basis? Is there an associated cost you need to add to your list of monthly outgoings? It's always great if you can create a driveway or extend one, as this can be a real selling point later. I once bought a place in a road where the residents' society had decided only visitors were allowed to park on the road. Everyone else had a space in a small block around the corner. That was fine if you didn't have kids, get injured...or get old!

Go with your gut

Go back as many times as you need – don't be afraid to make a nuisance of yourself. It's a lot to expect someone to spend hundreds of thousands of pounds and potentially the rest of their life somewhere having only looked at it for half an hour. Take this list with you and until you can answer all points you're not ready to make a decision. You can download one of these lists from my blog www.TheHomeGenie.com

Ask yourself though does it feel right as well? There's no point it being perfect on paper if it just ain't right in your bones. I can sometimes come across as being pretty heartless when it comes to homes, but I *do* fall in love as well. I always think houses have personalities and you either click, you don't, or you can learn to love them. Whilst I'm trying to help you to move up the ladder as quickly as possible, I also recognise that life is short and you need to love your home even if it isn't your forever home.

Ask the agent

If the homeowner is present at the viewing, ask them as many questions as you can as it's always best to hear it from the horse's mouth. Although, don't always just take their answers as gospel. I once asked the owner of a house I was viewing what the metal jack was for (when it was clearly holding up the dilapidated porch). As his nose grew he replied that it was just somewhere to store it!

Agents are there to sell the house though. So although you aren't directly their client, they want things to move as quickly as possible so will want to answer your questions. Or good agents will anyway.

There are a number of questions you should absolutely ask as well. Here's a handy list.

✓ How long has it been on the market?
✓ Is this the first time to market by this particular vendor?!
✓ Have they had any sales fall through, and if so what was the reason?
✓ Why are they selling?
✓ Are there any management fees?
✓ If its leasehold, how long is the lease on it?
✓ Have there been any neighbour disputes?
✓ Have they ever been refused planning permission?

✓ Do they have the planning permission for any extensions or a loft conversion?

✓ If it's rented out what is the monthly income?

A lot of this will be addressed by the conveyancing solicitor, but I don't want to have got that far down the line before I get these answers.

Open-house viewings

An open-house situation is where all viewings of a property are expected to be in one day or a weekend. These are rarely going to go in favour of the buyer. It's a tactic used to create a buzz and sense of urgency. They are commonly used on properties the agent expects to be in high demand, particularly when it's a seller's market. What can happen is buyers feel the rush to offer that day, or even get into a bidding war with another buyer. It doesn't always happen though and sometimes they fall flat on their face! If you're bidding against others it's unlikely you will be getting the best price for a place.

To do list

- Create your viewings spread sheet or log book
- Use my 'property with potential' check list against properties you find
- Book your viewings
- Download my 'viewing' check list from www.TheHomeGenie. com and follow to the letter
- Enlist a builder to come with you for the second viewing
- Get all your questions answered

CHAPTER 8:
Making an offer
to moving in

Making an offer – choose with your heart, but buy with your head

Oh if only I had a penny for every time someone told me with a pained face that their offer had been rejected and they're now waiting with baited breath for the agent to come back with a response to an elevated offer. They don't know if they should chase…noooooooooooooooooooo I scream for two reasons!!!

A. Don't chase as the last thing you want is for anyone to get a whiff of your desperation. It's like a new fragile relationship and you want to be the one treating them mean to keep them keen – we all know what happens to the one on the other end!

B. You've clearly fallen in love too early. You've barely dated. You've not even got to second base (do people say that anymore?). Yet you're picking out the wedding dress!!!!

When you make a decision about something that is costing you an extraordinary amount of money you need to do it with your head, not your heart. You may love the character of the house, the location, the fact it has oodles of potential, but you need to strip the emotion before you commit to stripping the walls. Often, time becomes the issue. You've been house-hunting for too long. You've had your heart set on settling down. Just as this is not a good reason to settle for the wrong guy or girl, it's certainly not a good enough reason to rush into pouring your life-savings into a money pit.

Get all the costings down on paper so you know what your absolute upper limit is before this becomes an emotional buy. This should take into account how much the renovations will cost and how much it will be worth at the end. Have you made sure your exit plan is also satisfied? If you pay this uppermost figure will lodgers, Airbnb guests, or tenants be enough to cover your mortgage payments if things get tricky? Commit by writing down on a piece of paper that if you can't buy it for that amount that you will walk away, knowing you have made the right decision. I have missed out on houses on a number of occasions. I have had to delete the agent's number from my phone to stop myself from drunk texting a higher offer (this is a joke of course!). Each time, it turned out to be a lucky escape because someone, I mean somewhere better came along.

Deciding how much to offer

Working out how much to offer is like playing a game of *Cluedo*. Hopefully you have been collecting some of the evidence from your chats with the agent and vendor. You know if they are in a hurry or not, whether or not there's competition, and it should have been indicated to you if they are likely to accept below the asking price as well. Here's a little guide to the terminology used when it comes to asking prices:

Guide price = an indication of the owner's expectations. It allows flexibility so that with interest it could go up, or allows room for negotiation.

Offers in the region of = could be higher or lower. As it says really, but is trying to be less intimidating.

Asking price = what the owners are asking for (the agent won't necessarily agree, and of course they know the market better).

Offers in excess of = as it says and is usually driven by the vendor hoping for more than it's worth. So the agent says to get more viewings let's go for a slightly lower price, but say we want more. Doesn't mean you can't offer below, but the psychology of these terms can be incredibly powerful and so you may have competitors thinking they have to offer above.

Your offer must reflect the following factors:

-   How much you have to spend (taking into account stamp duty,

solicitors fees, moving costs and very importantly renovation costs).
- How much other similar properties in relative states have gone for in that area recently.
- How much it will cost to improve that property to then make a profit if you were to sell (no point in breaking even).

So there is research online, with local estate agents, builders and other home improvement experts to be done here. Always add at least 10% to whatever you think things will cost.

So you know your maximum price you can go to, but you shouldn't be nose-diving straight in at that of course! You also don't want to be laughed at – you risk not being taken seriously. This is something you need to think carefully about. Also plan the increments you will go up in if you are forced to increase the offer.

A personal need to rush should never be a reason to go above the limit you have set. If you already own a property and don't want to keep your buyers waiting, have you considered selling and renting short-term? Yes it's a bit more hassle, but only a bit more and could put you at the front of the queue for the best properties, as you become a chain-free buyer. If you're a first-time buyer but you now have your heart set on moving and settling down, you need to have a word with yourself as there is too much emotion going into your decision making.

Making the offer

It may help to get your mortgage agreed in principle at this stage, so you can show the agent you're ready to move on this ASAP. If you're confident from a previous meeting with a mortgage broker that you will get one for this amount it isn't totally necessary, but you should at least have all the paperwork ready. If there is likely to be a lot of competition for the property though, having the Agreement in Principle makes you more attractive as a buyer.

How do you make the offer though? Well first you pour yourself a neat whiskey…only joking. I'm more of a sparkling wine girl. Seriously though you have a chat with yourself, is what you do first.

You get into character. You are a hard-nosed property investor who is about to make an offer they will accept. Have a script in front of you if it helps your confidence. You then pick up the phone to the agent, or the vendor if dealing with them directly.

Above all, make sure you are as cool as a cucumber. You're not in a hurry, and you're not in a hurry to hear an answer either. So take a deep breath and pick up the phone. Build rapport by asking the agent or vendor about something personal you picked up last time, like 'how was the wife's 40th?', 'did little Bobby get into the school they were hoping for?', erm 'how's the dog?' etc. It then helps to summarise what influenced your decision. Pardon the language, but you may have heard of the 'shit sandwich'? Start with a positive piece of bread, like say the location is what drew you to this property. The meat in the middle is the information you picked up by using my awesome viewing checklist. Air your concerns about traffic noise, damp issues, redecoration needed etc. You are showing yourself to be intelligent and savvy and not to be taken for a ride. Then the bread on top is how you put your offer forward, with positive terminology. 'Even with all that in mind, I'm happy to offer xxx'. If you're chain free or a cash buyer, it's worth reminding them of this, and the fact you are happy to move at their pace. Then you shut up. No really, you go silent and listen. Really listen to see if the agent is giving anything away. The reaction may be a guffaw followed by 'I'm not even going to insult my client by putting that to them' – which they are obliged to do no matter how 'silly', by the way. It's more likely they will say something like 'I'm not sure they will go for that, but I'll let you know what they say.' At this point you say, 'no problem, well you have my number' – remember, play it cool!

Then you go and down the rest of that whiskey! You try and forget about it. Remember we are trying to take the emotion out of this, and if you sit staring at your phone, when you pick it up on the first ring, like the desperado you are, the negotiator is going to smell that anxiety down the phone! So go for a walk, play squash, listen to your favourite music. Just find anything you can to distract your thoughts.

When you get the call, you take a moment to get into that cool as a cucumber persona again. Take a deep breath and answer casually.

If the offer has been accepted, there is still a way to go, so letting off party poppers is a bit keen and will come across as so! A 'matter of fact' response is required, talking about the next step, which may be something like arranging a survey.

If the offer is rejected, we go to stage two – which is a good thing as it means you didn't go in too high to start with! The agent will often 'advise' where to go to. He/she may well be on your side at this point as they just want this sale to happen. But there's also every chance they are playing you, as they are expert sales people at the end of the day. I will always listen to their recommendation but usually stick to my original plan, maybe with a little flexibility. Unless this really is now your very highest offer, you don't want to say so as then you will have egg on your face if you go up again. I wouldn't up my offer more than three times anyway as again they will stop taking you seriously. Remember if your highest offer is rejected you walk away with your head held high, knowing that you were in control and chose not to pay more than it was worth to you.

It may be that they come back saying that someone else has made an offer. Now this could be a little too coincidental, but you are never likely to find out how much truth there is in that, so you stick to your plan. Remember that although 'a few thousand' may not seem like a lot in the grand scheme of things when you're spending that kind of money, it could be the difference between affording a new kitchen and not. So don't get complacent about the fact we are talking hard earned (or hard borrowed!) pounds here.

Remember if you don't quite make it past the post right now, all is not lost. Keep an eye on that property. If it goes under offer with someone else but goes back to 'for sale' later, you can swoop in with another offer and the vendor may be more keen to sell this time around. If there's no movement for a couple of months remind the agent you are there.

You must insist that part of your offer is that the property is taken off the market and that no more viewings will be conducted. The last thing you need now as you get all your ducks in a row is to find a fox has come in and eaten the ducklings behind your back – I'll go more into what's known as 'gazumping' later.

Getting a mortgage

Now the offer has been accepted, you need your actual mortgage. So first on your list is to go back to your mortgage adviser, who will be very happy to hear from you! If you listened to me earlier you should have all the relevant information at your fingertips and now they will need to see it.

Surveys

Your lender will need to have the house valued before it's a done deal. This is essentially to work out if the property is worth what you are planning to pay for it. They need to know that if everything goes pear shaped that they will recoup their costs by selling the property.

You may think you have got a good deal on the place you're buying, but don't be disappointed if the valuation comes back bang on the amount you have offered. They don't tend to come up with a figure greater than the offer you've made. The lender will want to use one of their preferred surveying companies to do this, but you will usually pay for it. Sometimes they will offer to cover the cost as part of your mortgage deal. You might be able to add this cost to your mortgage, but it is likely to be cheaper if you pay upfront. They can be eye-wateringly expensive, but I'm afraid you have no choice but to have one done if you are relying on a mortgage.

The survey is NOT going to tell you about the condition of the house though. Yep, there's more of your hard earned cash to go out if you want to know about the fabric of the property you're buying. This second survey, however, can be a strong bargaining chip as the defects it will more than likely come up with are reasons to renegotiate on the price, or to ask the vendor to fix. There are different levels of surveys, and depending on the state of the house, you will need to decide which one to go for – if at all. You may come across the term 'RICS' which stands for The Royal Institution of Chartered Surveyors. If your surveyor is registered with them they will have MRICS after their name and carry insurance to protect you if any mistakes are made. There are other qualifications recognised by the industry as well, such as Surveyors and Valuers Accreditation or SAVA.

Condition report

The most basic condition report will usually give you a traffic light indication of what needs attention around the property, highlighting any significant issues. It will not go into a huge amount of detail.

HomeBuyer's report

This will have a lot more detail and goes into issues such as damp and subsidence. This report will give you an idea of any necessary repairs and also anything that doesn't meet the current building regulations. It's worth pointing out that the surveyor will not move anything, or look under floorboards so it will only be a 'surface-level' inspection. This is only suitable for properties of conventional construction up to around 100 years old.

Building survey

This will only be undertaken on houses, not usually flats because of restricted access. The surveyor will really get stuck in with this one, checking behind light furniture and in the loft. You will get a very detailed report and some surveyors will include advice on how much time and money repairs will cost.

If you are following my model, it is likely you are buying a property that is more than 50 years old, and needs more than a lick of paint. Although this more thorough survey can be pricey, it can save you money in the long run. If it uncovers major issues you weren't aware of you will either be able to run for the hills or renegotiate – I'd probably advise the latter first!

In my experience, houses can be tricky. Sometimes they look like they might just about fall down, but actually the problems are relatively inexpensive. On the flipside they could seem in good nick, but remove that strategically placed chest of drawers and you uncover a whole load of trouble. It's worth shopping around as surveyor's costs can vary significantly, and will also depend on the location and size of the property. If you really can't stretch to one of these and you're buying an older property, at the very least you should take a trusted builder with you to view the house – no matter how knowledgeable you think you are!

Conveyancing

If you followed my advice, you will have found a solicitor, preferably recommended, early on so that as soon as your offer is accepted you can instruct them to start the conveyancing process. I can't stress enough the importance of getting a decent conveyancing solicitor – it's quite handy if they are local enough to you that you can march into their office as well if needs be! This can be an incredibly stressful and painfully slow part of the home buying journey. I think it's worse when you are selling as well as buying, so I will go into more detail later on. Things can feel like they are moving impossibly slowly as the relevant searches take time (sometimes 10-14 days from the local authority) and the solicitor is dependent on management or mortgage companies also getting back to them. Sometimes there is someone in the chain who needs things to go at a certain pace as well! It's not always your solicitor's fault, but they should be keeping the lines of communication open with you so you're not left in the dark.

When there is a chain involved it can be like trying to get monkeys into a barrel, so agreeing to a completion date for all involved can be very difficult. If you have gone through an agent, a good one should also be getting involved with all this to chase the other side – they want their commission remember, but they also deal with this process day in, day out and often know the lawyers. If you are selling on your own, you may find it harder to get answers from the seller's party and there can be a lot of fobbing off! When we come to the 'selling your home' section, I'll give you some pointers so you can have a modicum of control.

Your solicitor is basically carrying out the process of transferring ownership of the property. There are a number of checks that need to take place for this to happen, and they will be dealing with your vendor's solicitor as well. They will need to do checks and searches to make sure everything is in order – basically that you are buying what you think you are buying. Some of these checks are mandatory by law, some may be recommended by your solicitor. If you've had any niggling concerns, like boundary issues, access or a dodgy loft conversion, it's worth flagging with your solicitor rather than putting total faith in their experience. Remember it's unlikely they will ever even set foot in the property. Common issues are missing paperwork and in particular documents concerning alterations made to the property in the past. These may not have planning permission or building regulation certificates. What I would say is that once the sale goes through, these documents will belong to you. File them so you have them all to hand for when you come to sell and you will save everyone a lot of time! Also responding to emails, signing what needs to be signed, as promptly as possible will mean that *you* are not part of the problem!

One thing to make sure you are on top of is what is to be left at the property. If you've been told the white goods are included, make sure that's written in the contract, usually in a signed additional sheet of paper. If you don't want the rusty old banger in the front garden, make sure that is stipulated too!

In theory, it is possible to rush through the conveyancing process if you are in a hurry – in as little as a few days in fact. Both parties would have to be on board and on the ball though. There certainly wouldn't be time to do the relevant searches, and enquiries would be kept to a minimum. I'd ask what's the great hurry? It would be incredibly risky to buy a property without the usual investigation.

Gazumping, gazundering and gazanging

Gazumping
Considering how much money is involved in buying a house, it's quite incredible that you could have invested in surveys and solicitors, but if the vendor changes their mind – or gets a better offer – they can decide to ask for more money, or just pull out. This happens more often in a seller's market, when house prices are increasing rapidly. The sale can take such an age to go through (typically 10-12 weeks) the vendor realises that by exchange time

his product is now worth more than the original agreement. It may be that someone has come in and made a better offer, or I've known vendors to *declare* they've had a better offer to panic the buyer into matching it when I'm not sure that offer ever existed! This is all because we are just dealing in a verbal agreement until contracts are signed. In Scotland, local law dictates that a contract comes earlier, so gazumping happens far less often.

There are a couple of ways to avoid being gazumped. When you put in an offer to the agent you could state it is on the condition that the property is pulled from their website and window and a 'sold' sign put up immediately, rather than 'sold subject to contract', which means it's fair game until the contracts have been signed! This will reduce the amount of chancers thinking they can put an offer in anyway. Even more sure-fire is a 'lock-out agreement'. This is a pre-contract between the seller and buyer stating that the buyer has the exclusive right to buy the property within a certain period of time (usually around 12 weeks). There is an additional cost to having this drawn up, but can certainly be worth it in some situations.

Gazundering

'Gazundering' is when the buyer pulls a fast one and waits until just before contracts are signed to lower his/her offer – threatening to pull out and break a chain of several sales! I would never advise this unless something in the solicitor's search has brought to light a genuine reason to not pay the agreed price. Frankly it's just bad manners and underhand. If something disastrous happens during the sale that affects the property market drastically and you are going to pay more than market value for a property, I would consider renegotiating and even pulling out though. It is unfair and it doesn't leave a very nice taste in the mouth but you also don't want to be in danger of being in a negative equity situation. If you are going to do this, you need to calculate how much you will have lost in surveys and solicitors fees. There may be some compromise you can come to with the seller, rather than money and time being wasted. I'll go into more detail as to how you can avoid this happening to you when we look at selling, later in the book.

Gazanging

'Gazanging' is when a seller pulls out and takes the property off the market to wait until it picks up again when they might get a better price. If a vendor does threaten to pull out, do a lot of internal swearing and then tread carefully, always letting your head rather than your heart make the decisions. It's easy to convince yourself it's worth upping your offer rather than losing out. Remind yourself of the sums that brought you to the offer price in the first place. If there's wiggle room then fine, but don't be wiggling if the space is smaller than your hips! Also go with your gut. I have had this happen to me, I felt something was fishy, stood my ground and coincidentally the seller backed down! Good job I enjoy a game of poker eh?! Again the 'lock-out' agreement could avoid this happening.

If you are buying and selling at the same time and the vendor pulls out, I would seriously consider going through with the sale of your house (if you've done well of course) and renting. This may sound like a lot of hassle, but it takes the need for haste out of the whole situation, which puts the ball in your court. You then become a desirable chain-free buyer. Just be warned if you are in a steeply rising market this might not be such a good idea as your money in the bank from the sale of your house is unlikely to be rising at the same rate.

Exchange and completion

The signing of the contracts is a very exciting and nerve-wracking stage. There's no going back, but you can also sigh with relief as it's nearly all over. It's worth knowing that exchange can only take place when everyone, including the whole of the chain if there is one, agrees on a completion date. Once signed, no one can pull out. Completion is when the money will be transferred and you will be handed the keys. Sometimes exchange and completion can happen on the same day. If you are currently renting and have time left on your contract this can work, but if you try and coincide your last day of renting with exchange and completion, you may have a heart attack before you get there as things rarely run smoothly! Also you may have an unscrupulous vendor who takes advantage of the situation by asking for more money at the last minute. Do you see why I said earlier the imminent arrival of a baby is not the kind of deadline you want hanging over you in this situation?!

Make sure you have your deposit ready and waiting. Feel free to be a micro-manager over all the finer details. I heard of a heart stopping moment on completion day when funds were transferred to the solicitor, but promptly disappeared. It turned out there was one digit wrong with the sort code!

Once the contracts have been exchanged you will need to have buildings insurance. Yes that's right, you may not have moved in yet, but if the house burns down it's your responsibility aaaargh!

Making it through!

With all the will in the world it's likely the process of buying a house is going to be stressful. There are so many potential problems and people with their own agendas involved! At times you will feel very much out of control. If the only thing you can manage is your mental wellbeing then focus on that! When something happens that feels like it's catastrophic, remember we are just talking about bricks and mortar. Rather than internalising your frustration take a walk. Exercise deep breathing. Write down your thoughts and fears as they will always seem more manageable when on paper. If you are buying with a partner remember that communication is key during this time. You must work as a team, and if one side has concerns both should take them seriously.

If the worst happens and it all falls through, it can be devastating. But in my experience things turn out for the best and there are always plenty more fish in the sea. This is why it's so crucial to keep level-headed about the whole sale as heated emotions don't do anyone any favours.

'Remember that not getting what you want is sometimes a wonderful stroke of luck'
Dalai Lama

Preparing to move

As I've already mentioned, I have moved homes 28 times in my life. Some people find this incredibly stressful, but I consider myself a pro so have it down to a fine art! It may seem odd that I'm devoting any pages to this at all, but if all goes according to plan you will be moving a few times over the next several years, so it's worth getting a system in place. Here's what you need to do:

Set up a mail redirection

This can be done online at www.royalmail.com/personal/receiving-mail/redirection/ – I would do this for the maximum allowed of 12 months as it's amazing how time flies, particularly when you've just moved in.

Keep an address change list

This will be handy for further moves and will enable you to keep track of what you have and haven't updated. Here are some you may want on your list:

Bank accounts
Mortgage provider
ISAs
Credit cards
Loan providers
The company you work for
Council tax
HMRC
National insurance
TV licence
TV provider (eg Sky, BT)
Car registration
Driving licence
Car insurance
Mobile network provider
Landline provider
Electricity supplier
Water supplier
Gas supplier
Internet provider

Accountants
Life insurance
Dentist
Doctors
Health insurance
Pet insurance
Vets
Club memberships
Online supermarket accounts
Reward cards (easily forgotten, but you don't want to miss out on those Boots points!)
Avios and other schemes

Also make sure you have a forwarding address for the vendor. If you have to continue to deal with their post for more than a year and after polite requests they don't seem to be doing anything about it you might want to write 'return to sender' on the original unopened envelope, with a note telling the sender the new address. If you don't have a forwarding address, add 'address unknown'. You shouldn't have to pay for this by the way.

Book a removal van

If you don't have many possessions you may be able to do a simple move by car – always rope family or friends in to help! Any larger furniture will necessitate a van. Although you will pay a bit more I always think it's worth getting a man/woman and a van. It can be back-breaking work carrying endless boxes backwards and forwards, up and down, when you aren't used to doing it. I actually ended up with a sciatica problem from one of my many moves because I tried to do it on my own! If you are looking to move on a Saturday, you will need to book ASAP as they can be in demand. I would advise you move on a weekday though as it makes life easier regarding solicitors, and also getting the keys off the agent.

You could go for the extravagant option of using a full packing and moving service. They come in and wrap, pack and move all of your possessions. Sounds tempting, but they charge a pretty penny and will never be as careful as you are. They have insurance to cover breakages, but personally I'd rather have everything in one piece. Also as you will see in the next section, if you know how and where everything has been packed it makes life so much easier at the other end.

Pack

OK so I'm really anal about this, but trust me it makes life so much easier. If you are doing up your new abode it may be that you even need to keep some boxes unopened for a while or even in storage, so the more organised you are the less frustration you will have to endure over the coming months. Yes you can get specialist packing boxes, but these tend to be big and bulky. It makes them hard to manoeuvre as there's a tendency to overfill them. When you come to unpack it's difficult to see the wood for the trees when you have boxes piled high. Instead it's worth investing in a number of the 'bags for life' from the supermarket. I'm not talking about the plastic ones, but the large woven or canvas ones. They are cheaper than boxes and you can store them easily for the next move. Take care to pack these strategically and think about where they are going to go so you can clearly label them and they will be delivered straight to that room. This will save you time and energy. Some bigger items will need boxes, so it's worth asking around to see if anyone has some spare.

Oh and by the way, I start packing the minute an offer is accepted, rather than leaving it to the last minute. If you start packing items you rarely use, even if this sale falls through they will be ready for the next time. It's also a great opportunity to have a clear-out so you aren't moving unnecessary stuff that will just end up cluttering up your new place!

Moving from rental accommodation

If you are a first-time buyer it may well be you have the issue of sorting out your rental place. The last thing you want is to be paying a mortgage and rent, but it's not always easy to get dates to coincide. Don't be afraid to talk to your landlord about your situation. If your contract is likely to overlap, offer to take the hassle out of their hands by finding a replacement tenant yourself. At the end of the day they just want to make sure they don't have any void periods, so if you can sort this for them they should be happy. If you are looking for a replacement tenant it makes sense to present the rental place as if you were trying to sell it – so perhaps take some tips from the section on house dressing later in this book!

Of course if there is a delay in the exchange of contracts and you've timed it too neatly, you may find yourself without a roof over your head so it's best to give yourself a couple of week's grace. Always have a plan B of staying with family or friends in the interim period. Your vendor should also be keen to make this all work for you as they don't want the sale to fall through. If their property is empty could you even move in before completion and pay them rent? If you don't ask you don't get!

What to expect on moving day

The completion usually happens at midday to give enough time for the funds to be transferred. You will then need to pick up keys from the agent. Under usual circumstances you will not be allowed in until the funds have cleared. It is not uncommon to have the vendor carrying boxes out of the back door as the new owner carries their belongings in through the front door.

If you are buying a doer-upper, don't expect the property to have been left in a reasonable state. If they didn't clean it when they lived there, they certainly won't for you! I love seeing what treats have been left for us. One item that particularly springs to mind was a deep fat fryer…full of used oil! If there is just too much stuff left, you need to contact your solicitor, as items not taken should have been specified in the contract. You can then charge the cost of removing anything to the previous owner.

One of the first things you want to do is take meter readings and call up the providers to set up your name on the account. Don't forget to do the final readings on your previous property and close the accounts by the way. You can then notify them of the previous owner's forwarding address so they can pay off their final bills. If you don't do this immediately there could end up being a dispute you could do without at this time! Hopefully the vendor will have taken the readings themselves, but don't rely on them being this organised as it will become your problem.

It's worth finding out where the stop-tap is in case you need to turn the water off in an emergency. Finding where the fuse box is also makes sense as rooting around in the dark, in amongst your unpacked bags and boxes isn't much fun! If you had a reasonable vendor this is all something you could check with them in the weeks leading up to completion.

Everybody needs good neighbours

A top tip is to befriend your neighbours as soon as possible. If you are going to be doing improvements it may be disruptive for them so you want them to be onside. But on a more human level the relationship you have with your neighbour can shape your every day. I know the power of this as I have had both awesome and awful neighbours over the years. My dear friend Daphne even did a joint extension with us only months after meeting!

To do list

- Do your sums to work out how much you think the property is worth and will be worth once improved
- Work out the top price you are prepared to pay – and stick to it
- Possibly get an AIP before making the offer, but this is not essential
- Put together your negotiation plan
- Script your offer conversation
- Celebrate (only a little bit) once offer has been accepted
- Start the mortgage ball rolling
- Arrange your mortgage survey
- Arrange any other necessary surveys
- Instruct a recommended conveyancing solicitor
- Make a note of anything to be included in the sale
- Send any relevant notes and concerns to your solicitor
- Practise deep breathing in times of stress

- Arrange building insurance for when you've exchanged
- Set up mail redirection
- Make an address change list and do any you can before you move
- Get a forwarding address from the vendor
- Leave a forwarding address at your previous property
- Book a removal van if necessary and see if friends can help
- Stock up on 'bags for life'
- Ask friends, colleagues and family for any spare removal boxes
- Start packing and label those bags and boxes!
- If renting, speak to your landlord about potential flexibility
- Unpack – but if you're doing major work on the property keep less urgent items packed away

PART 2

IMPROVING YOUR HOME

CHAPTER 9
Planning home improvements

Where to start

So you've unpacked as much as you can and you're sitting there thinking 'well what now?' The excitement of collecting the keys can certainly last less time than the smell of damp, dogs, and nicotine left behind by the previous owner. You want to pre-empt that lull in energy and motivation by getting stuck in with improvements straight away. You would be amazed how easily you can get used to certain things and not see the need to rush anymore. Before you know it, weeks turn into years and you're sat in a worse house than the one you bought. It's time to get planning. Well, actually, I would argue that you want to start the planning well before you collect the keys!

Vision board

A vision board can be a great way to get ideas down and drum up some motivation. Go through some interiors magazines or sites online and cut or print out anything that takes your fancy that you feel could work with your new place. Pinterest.co.uk and Houzz. co.uk are great sites to give you some ideas. This is just a vision board, we are not necessarily expecting the finished house to look like this, but it is there to keep us going through the darker moments, so make it as captivating as you can. Place this somewhere you can see it every day to keep the dream at the front of your mind.

What you want v. what actually adds value

Whilst the vision board is there to excite, we don't want to go overboard in reality. Chances are there isn't the budget to anyway. It can almost be better to be restricted by a smaller purse believe it or not. The amount of times I hear excited homeowners talk about having improved their house by adding a hot tub, a dome skylight or a hand-made kitchen. Yes of course they have improved their home in their eyes, and if it's their forever home then good for them. Improving to satisfy your personal preferences doesn't always mean adding value, or at least adding enough value to justify the amount they've spent.

Part of your planning needs to include some due diligence. Speak to local estate agents about what your target market will be once you've finished your works. Ask what do buyers for this type of property tend to ask for on their wish list? What do the masses find appealing about certain homes? If a similar house on your road or in the area has been renovated and sold well, go and have a nose – that can be one of the easiest ways to decide what you should do. If it has stuck on the market for a while, still have a nose – just see if you can work out what they've done wrong so you don't make the same mistake.

Home improvement to do list

I know not everyone likes a 'to do' list, but I think it's essential if you are to work your way through this project. Go through each room and assess what needs to be done to make it acceptable, and then to really enhance it. If the budget is tight it might make sense to concentrate on one room at a time, but bear in mind that you may be able to save costs on things like carpet if you are doing several rooms at a time.

Part of your 'to do' list should cover who you can delegate certain tasks to. What can you have a go at yourself – anyone can rip up old carpet for example? Do you have a friend or relative who is a bit handy and only too happy to help? There will be certain aspects you need to get a professional in to do. I'll guide you on these delegation decisions as I go through each aspect of the project.

See your 'to do' list as a tally of milestones, as opposed to an essay of chores, and it will help to prevent precious time being wasted through procrastination. If you can break down any jobs even further then do so, we want to make these manageable baby steps as they are far more likely to be completed without hesitation if they seem less daunting.

Funding improvements

When you were working out how much you had to spend on buying the property, the home improvement budget should have also been factored in of course. If you don't have enough for your plans it might be worth getting a loan. Bear in mind this is further debt so should only be entertained if you're as certain as you can be that you will be able to recoup costs, including the interest, when you come to sell. Obviously this certainty only comes from thorough research, and borrowing more is to be avoided where possible.

Doing as much of the home improvements as you can yourself will obviously help to reduce costs. My husband and I have always roped our very handy parents in too! But also staggering the work so you can save up for each stage might make it easier. As you create your 'to do' list include your calculations for each item so you can work out an affordable payment plan. It may be that you can find other ways to help fund improvements, like having a lodger for a while or Airbnb guests to build up some extra cash. Remember the lifestyle choices we talked about earlier in the book to help with savings? Now you're actually in your place, the incentive to tame a few unnecessary spending habits will be even stronger. Along those lines, if there's anything you are getting rid of in the house think about how you might be able to sell it. We had to replace a boiler once because it wasn't appropriate for the house and somebody was still happy to pay £300 for the old one – it all adds up and is better off being used than going to landfill. In fact it is always my policy to reuse, recycle or sell whatever I possibly can when renovating – at the very least it saves on skip space!

Live in amongst the mess?

We've done this time and time again. Our most recent project was the first one we moved out for, partly because it was uninhabitable with no electricity, and partly because our baby was due in the middle of it all, so it wasn't the ideal 'nesting' environment.

The benefit of living at the site is you can keep an eye on what is going on if you have builders in! If you're doing a lot of the work yourself you are more likely to do the odd job here and there as you have a daily 'in your face' reminder! Do expect there to be a lot of dust. Don't expect to be able to keep on top of the mess – it's pointless and if you accept defeat at the start it will be a lot less stressful. Be warned if you have builders in they tend to rip everything out at the start so you are unlikely to have some of the most basic amenities. It might be worth having this chat to see if it's actually necessary for them to do this! I have spent months without a shower or even a basin in our only bathroom (frankly, I felt fortunate to have a toilet!).

It's a luxury to be able to afford both the rent and mortgage of course. In the early days of renovating houses every penny counted and I preferred to put any cash into the improvements. Renting is expensive, let alone when you are paying a mortgage as well. But renting short term can be even more expensive. Maybe a compromise is to stick it out for as long you can and then rely on the kindness of friends and family for a week or so when it gets to crunch time when even the toilet has been ripped out! If you don't have those options it is likely to be cheaper to find a local Airbnb host for a couple of weeks rather than a short-term rental for a few months.

If you have kids I think it is a bit of a game-changer as you need to make sure they are safe. If there is a lot of dust it can be more dangerous to their tiny lungs. There may be lethal tools left around. You try stopping crawling babies and toddlers from going where they shouldn't! If they are older though, I think an experience of going back to basics can be very good for them. Our children are living in a world that crumbles when the Wi-Fi goes down and it won't harm them to appreciate the mod cons they have come to take for granted. Let's call it character building. They may even learn something that will serve them well when they follow in your footsteps in the future! If they are at exam age it might be worth arranging a desk space at a friend's or neighbour's so they are able to concentrate.

Identifying urgent problems

There will be some necessary works that you need to get done sooner rather than later. If you had a building survey, this should have all been highlighted, but the surveyor will not always have total access to everything at the time. Getting a trusted builder in as soon as possible will help you to assess this. Whilst it would be nice to get everything done in one go (and tends to be cheaper overall) I understand that your budget might not stretch to that. The decorating may just have to wait whilst you spend your cash on fixing a damp problem. Some issues will just get worse and more expensive to fix if left alone. If you prioritise the pretty stuff you will no doubt end up having to redecorate later anyway, costing you double.

The first place to start is the roof because if that is not fixed you will be fighting a losing battle. Here are the urgent issues to look out for:

- Roof issues
- Damp
- Woodworm
- Dry and wet rot
- Cracks in render
- Mould
- Unsafe ceilings

It's unlikely you will be able to fix these problems yourself and will need to get professionals in. By doing so you can also get the appropriate certificates to show it has been done, which you should then file away ready for when you sell. If your future buyer's survey comes up with any of the above as potential problems you can prove you have fixed them and that they are not a reason to lower your price.

Electrics

If you're buying an older property, the likelihood is that you will need to update the electrics. You want to get this all done first to avoid having to redecorate later on. Besides, if the electrics aren't up to modern standards they could be in a dangerous state. Getting in a qualified electrician to do this is a no-brainer. They will be up-to-speed on current building regulations and will be able to provide you with the necessary certificates...which of course you file away ready for when you come to sell! Be warned that if you are having rewiring done it will probably make more of a mess than you might expect.

Plumbing

Plumbing may not be quite as urgent, but there are a few checks you can do yourself to assess the timescale you need to work to.

-   I mentioned in 'Savvy house-hunting' about central heating and if there is none, this should absolutely go on your list. There's no point in doing some great improvements to a place but then trying to sell it without central heating, as the house simply won't reach its potential value.
-   If the boiler looks old and uncared for this will probably need immediate attention. Its service history should have been given to you during the sale. If it shows a strong history, make sure you continue this using a Gas Safe registered engineer and keep the paperwork filed away for when you sell – broken record?! Trust me you will thank me for my filing tips later on!
-   Check all radiators to see if they are leaking at all. There may be water stains, signs of rust, mould and low water pressure is also an indicator.
-   What you don't want, for your health and that of future residents, are lead water pipes. You can check these by scratching the surface and if it's shiny you will want to get them replaced.
-   Check there's a tight lid on the water tank and that it has adequate insulation around it, which you will often find in the loft. If not you could be at risk of contracting Legionnaires disease. If the property has been out of use for a while you will also want to flush it all through as dormant water, particularly if it's mixed with rust and debris, can be a breeding ground for Legionella.

If you are replacing an old boiler for a new combi or similar, bear in mind that you will probably need to change the old radiators as well as they are likely to be shedding particles and sediment into the system. Before changing an old boiler, make sure it's really necessary as they should last quite some time. From a fuel efficiency point of view, the newer boilers are better, but if you won't be staying at the property for too many years to come and it's running without a problem now, your money might be better spent elsewhere as you are unlikely to benefit from the cost savings if you're only there for a short time.

Having said that, a new boiler can be a strong selling point and is likely to also positively affect your EPC rating. Going forward this will become more important as there is talk of tax saving initiatives for more energy efficient properties, and I believe we should all be doing our bit where and when we can.

If it all seems in good order and there's just a weak shower you aren't keen on, you could save yourself a fortune by getting an eco shower head that uses air to add power to the water. I've used this many times and it really does work on the most dribbly of showers, and saves water at the same time. If you have any doubts though, you should get a plumber or a trusted builder in to give their opinion as it will cost less in the long run if you do the plumbing before decorating.

To do list

- Put together a vision board for your home
- Identify urgent problems
- Write your home improvement 'to do' list
- Consult with a builder to get an idea of costs
- Work out an affordable payment plan for your improvements
- Arrange for somewhere to stay short term for when things get too tough

Example of staircase opened up

CHAPTER 10:
Structural improvements

Reconfiguring

Every time I look at a house I can't help but work out how the layout could be better. I've seen some very strange configurations and can't help but wonder why someone would have come up with them in the first place.

Hopefully when viewing the property you were already tapping the walls to see which would easily come down to make an open plan space, but before you commit to anything, make sure the cost will be worth it. I've known people to swap a bedroom and a bathroom over just because they thought it would be better that way round. They didn't gain space or extra rooms, just an unnecessary works bill. I looked at a house once where the owner was very pleased with herself for having moved the staircase. I agree it probably did look better, and improved the flow, but it was a massive expense that would have barely touched on increasing the value of the house. If a staircase is blocked in and could be opened up, or an out-dated banister could be modernised, then this might be a more savvy way to spend your budget. Whilst we are on the subject of staircases, if the space underneath hasn't been used then there's an easy improvement straight away. Whether it's a much-needed extra toilet, or simply a storage cupboard for coats, shoes or vacuum cleaners, make use of it!

There are times when reconfiguring really does make sense. For example in one house I renovated there were seven bedrooms and two bathrooms, both of which were enough for merely a bath, a basin and a toilet. It was a Victorian house and they had obviously just been squeezed into a corridor at a later date. It was a very easy decision to steal some space from a larger than necessary adjacent bedroom to create a really spacious family bathroom. The important fact here was that the reduced room was still a healthy size double bedroom at the end of it, with its own window.

Bathroom before renovation

Bathroom knocked through to bedroom

Finished bathroom

Here are some opportunities you may want to look out for when it comes to reconfiguring:

A room off a room
This can really dampen appeal, so if you can find a way to create separate entrances, you're onto a winner.

Open-plan living space
It's more preferable these days to have open-plan reception areas, and these can create a lot more light, so knocking through can really make a property a lot more desirable.

Separate toilet
These are considered old fashioned now, so if you can fit one in the bathroom instead and use the extra space to turn a box room into a double bedroom, this will be worth doing. You might even be able to create a desirable ensuite.

Always be mindful of how much people will be prepared to pay for a property. Any improvement may increase the appeal, but a house will always have a ceiling when it comes to the amount people are happy to pay in that area. At the end of the day a 3-bedroom house has a top market value, no matter how much you've spent on it.

Extending

When we were at the viewing stage we were looking at properties with potential and in particular with the possibility to add square footage. There are many ways you can do this, and if you can't afford to have the work done yourself, even just getting any necessary planning permission can add value to your property.

Here are some of the ways you can add those extra metres:

Loft conversion
This is a relatively cheap way to add a room, and can be done quite quickly too. If you are including an ensuite it will push the price up, but if you're adding a room and there's only one bathroom in the house you might want to consider this. If you stick to certain guidelines you may not need planning permission as it is

considered permitted development, but you will need to adhere to building regulations. If you want extra space you might want to add a dormer, which may need permission. You will have hopefully done your homework before putting your offer in and had a look at what other houses on the street have done. If a neighbour with a dormer has set a precedent, it makes it easier for you to follow suit. Remember you will lose a bit of space on the floor below the loft to allow for the stairs.

Extension

Extending out the back or side can be a way to add space on multiple floors. Ideally you want to be creating an extra bedroom, although in London value tends be based on the square footage of a property. Consider the effect of light on the existing property, as extending can sometimes zap natural rays, making it less appealing. You may not need planning permission for this. Under certain conditions it will fall under the permitted development category, so long as you are not in a conservation area. Again looking at what neighbours have done can give you ideas and a sense of what the council is likely to allow.

There may be considerations to take into account, such as are there access points for any amenities in the way – check for manholes? If it is close to your neighbours, particularly if it is a terraced house, you may also need a Party Wall Agreement. Bungalows can be goldmines because if you have the money and can get the permission you can build upwards and outwards as they tend to have a decent amount of land around them. Make sure you aren't just extending for the sake of extending though. If it makes the house layout strange or darker you may make it less appealing than before.

Cellar conversion

If the property already has an unused cellar it feels like an easy decision to convert this into an extra bedroom. I have seen some shockers though! It is not as straightforward as you might think. Remember cellars were originally meant to store fruit and vegetables before the days of our beloved fridge-freezers – not exactly ideal bedroom conditions! They are quite often damp which can be costly to fix. Look out for wet floors as the water table may be a problem.

You are also likely to be lacking natural light. I'm not saying it's not worth doing, but you will need to do it well so make sure the cost is worth what you will gain in value.

Garage conversion

What do most people keep in their garage? If they have a drive it's not usually cars but junk they fill their garage with. This is valuable space that can be converted to add extra square footage. If it's not an appropriate location for a bedroom then a snug can be a real selling point for today's family buyer. You won't necessarily need planning permission, but you will need to satisfy building regulations.

Conservatory

Ask my mum about this one! She will tell anyone who is prepared to listen that she would never have a conservatory again! It was actually already there when she bought the house, but she found that it darkened the adjacent lounge. It was too hot in the summer and too cold in the winter to sit in anyway and the upkeep was expensive and time consuming. She is right in one respect that a conservatory doesn't always work, but it can be a way of adding space, it just needs to be done in the right way and is only suitable for certain properties. For one thing, if it looks like it's just been stuck on it's not going to enhance the selling power of the house. Some people love a conservatory though. If the flooring can flow from the house into it, that can make it feel more like an extension than a bolt-on. Have my mum's opinion in mind though, because if there isn't heating in there it is likely to make the adjacent room darker, and colder if you have the doors open to it. It should be permitted development so long as it abides by certain conditions and isn't in a conservation area. Again remember to check with local demand if this will actually add value before you splash the cash.

Overdeveloping

Before you get excited about adding space, be careful not to spend money on cramming as much in as possible to what was originally meant to be a much smaller home. The cash you put in to a house always has to be a lot less than the value added. Don't expect a

4-bedroom, 1-bathroom house you couldn't swing a cat in to fetch the same as the purpose built 4-bedder down the road, as you may waste a lot of time and money. I have a perfectly good loft space I could convert, but it's already a 7-bedroom house at the top end of the market, so I have to ask how many people will want that extra square footage. But hopefully none of this will be news to you as you will have done your due diligence before you even put an offer in right?!!

All your current planning questions should be answered at www. PlanningPortal.co.uk.

To do list

- Work out how you can gain more space or a better layout by reconfiguring, extending and/or converting
- Look into the local demand to see if these are worth doing
- Check the Planning Portal for allowances and restrictions

CHAPTER 11:
Getting the work done

Can you really DIY?

I loooove a bit of DIY...when it's going well! Seriously though I do understand that for some people the idea of picking up a screwdriver brings them out in a cold sweat. But if the budget is tight and you want to make money on your home you will have to get over this. You will be pleasantly surprised how easy and satisfying some minor jobs can be...really I promise! This does come with a caveat though as a bad DIY job sticks out like a sore thumb (usually caused by a wayward hammer!). So tread wisely and be obsessive about preparation. Also know when to give up and hand over to professionals before you're in too deep, as by then it may cost more to correct.

Most prep work you can do yourself. Removing wallpaper can be very satisfying, depending on how many layers there are. It's worth investing in a wallpaper steamer for about £30 and scrapers with replaceable blades, as this will cut down your time immensely. It's common for people to just wallpaper over wallpaper over wallpaper...so in older properties you can expect a few layers. You are also likely to have to contend with woodchip paper. Don't be tempted to just leave these as it will affect the appeal when you come to sell and I don't see it coming back into fashion any time soon!

I'm afraid you may find that in older houses the wall crumbles away with the paper as it's removed, particularly if it's still the original lath and plaster. If this happens, and in older properties you should expect it to, you will need to redo the walls with new plasterboard I'm afraid. If your budget really is tight and the wallpaper just needs a lick of paint, a simple tap will tell you the state of the wall underneath – a dull sound means it's seen better days and you won't want to hang pictures on it.

If you are painting or having the walls painted, they will need to be prepped after removing the paper as there are likely to be dents and uneven patches. I go into more detail on this later as this is something else you don't need to pay someone else to do. If you're painting woodwork this will need to be sanded lightly to get a 'key' so the fresh paint adheres. If the old paint is peeling you will need to remove any loose bits to get the desired lasting finish. Don't be tempted to skimp on this as 'shabby chic' doesn't appeal to everyone and can end up just looking shabby. I always think it's worth having a go at decorating so long as you have decent brushes, rollers and a steady hand. I give a comprehensive guide shortly, but if this really scares you then it might be worth getting in a professional.

If you hire the appropriate machine, sanding original floors can be hard work, but well worth it. Just make sure you try out stain samples before you finish the whole room, as the age of the wood will very much affect the colour you achieve.

Laying laminate or engineered wood flooring can also be done by your own fair hands – I even have a video to show you how on my website www.TheHomeGenie.com. Make sure you follow instructions to the letter and, once more, having the right tools is essential.

Unless you really have the proper training plumbing and electrics must be done by professionals. You could end up with serious, and even fatal, problems if you try to have a stab at these. If you are going to sell in the future, always have in mind that you need a good finish for it to be safe and have the appropriate certification. Cutting corners at the expense of these key factors will never serve you well in the long run and will more than likely come back to bite you, if not when you're living there then certainly when you come to sell.

Top 3 DIY tips

My main three tips when it comes to DIY are prepare thoroughly, get the right tools and dedicate enough time.

Preparation
It's always the most painstaking, boring and usually lengthy part of any DIY project but if you don't put in the preparation, you

won't get a decent finish, or at least a finish that lasts. But I also class things like putting down dustsheets, reading instructions and doing your online 'how to' research as key preparation ingredients.

The right tools
You don't need to invest a lot of money, but a basic tool kit is essential. If you can't borrow more pricey tools then you can usually hire them for a reasonable amount of money and it will save you a lot of time.

Enough time
How long is long enough?! Well I've learned to plan for things to take at least 50% longer than I expected. You want to make sure you put aside more than enough time as there's nothing more frustrating than not being able to finish a project when you're in the middle of it. By the same token, you never want to rush anything as that's when mistakes are made and will take longer to repair – trust me I speak from very bitter experience! You can always find guidance for DIY tasks online and www.TheHomeGenie.com also offers timing expectations for many projects.

Finding a builder and getting the best out of them

Poor old builders get a bad rap. Unfortunately in a number of cases that reputation is well deserved, as there are too many cowboys around. I think that even with the good ones a breakdown in communication and unrealistic expectations, from both sides, can lead to frustration and clashes! Oh I've fallen out with many builders over the years, and I accept it wasn't *all* of their fault *all* of the time. I have now found one I trust and to whom I can talk – and he listens too! Doug Reynolds is his name and he has taught me a lot about what to expect from a decent builder, but also how to be a decent client, which is key. So how do you find the good ones? Here's my guide to getting the right guys and gals for the job.

Get the *right* recommendation
100% you want to get recommendations when taking on a builder, but getting the *right* recommendation is just as important. With one big project it quickly became clear I had the wrong builder when he

advised me to rip down ceilings with original Victorian cornices and ceiling roses, to merely replace them with plasterboard. Foolishly we had found him courtesy of someone who'd had an extension on a modern place, which just wasn't comparable. I also think he was obviously better at managing smaller projects. Unfortunately the builder I had wanted to use, who was experienced in large Victorian houses, wasn't available straight away. Like a fine wine though, sometimes they are worth the wait! Even when a builder does come recommended you still want to do your own due diligence on them. Always look at some of their other completed work. If they're reluctant to show you then alarm bells should start to ring.

Get at least 3 quotes

You will be amazed at how much they vary! By the way you want a quote, rather than an estimation, which can be plucked out of the sky. A quote should come with all the paperwork, specification documents and plans. It is likely the costs along the way will change, as houses have a habit of coming up with surprises, and *you* may also change your mind about things. But if you know what's included at the start and you agree that you have to approve added extras along the way it should prevent any unnecessary tension – or surprises at the end.

The more thorough you can be with the information about what you are expecting, the easier it will be for the builder to give you an accurate quotation. Do your research beforehand to get a rough idea of how much you want to do should cost so you can make sure you are being realistic. I am always wary when asked the question 'what's your budget?' as I can't help but feel their quote will be tailored accordingly! In some cases though, the builder needs to check that the client's expectations are realistic for their budget, otherwise lots of time is wasted putting together a quote. Also ask the question 'what are the potential issues we could come across and how much will they cost to remedy?' and write it down! Obviously there are always likely to be some that nobody can predict, otherwise wouldn't life be simple?!

Don't expect the quote to come through within a day. It actually takes a lot of work, and therefore cost to the builder, to put one together and builders are rarely sat in front of computers, so do bear with them. You will probably expect me to say go for the cheapest quote. That's how I started out, but time and time again I was disappointed as extras were added on, corners cut and the builder's interest waned towards the end of a project. Some have a strategy to go in cheap to win the job and then sneak in extras, which the client will then feel compelled to pay. If you have thorough quotations you should be able to compare like-for-like and if one has an item that's missed on another you can bring that up and ask for it to be added.

Check the paperwork
Make sure your builder is using qualified tradesmen. All professionals on the job should come with the appropriate certification. Electrics, gas and structural work must be inspected and signed off correctly. If you don't get the appropriate paperwork, the problem will show itself when you come to sell the house – if not before! There should be no issue with you bringing this up at the start. Use a contract to protect both parties.

Set a budget and deadline – obviously!
This should go without saying! If neither you nor your builder has a timeframe and budget in mind, the sky's the limit...in a bad way! If you have gone for an itemized quote then that is the agreed budget with the builder. It's wise to always set your actual budget at 10-20% above that so you have room to move. If the build or renovation throws up an expensive problem you don't want to be forced into cutting corners, or not being able to finish the job. Your security blanket is best kept close to your chest though. If your builder knows there's more cash available it's just human nature to work to that upper limit.

Your builder should give you an expected timeframe, but in my experience you will want to add about 50% on top of that. At least then if they come in early it will be a pleasant surprise. It's worth establishing at the start whether or not that deadline is based on the whole team working on it every weekday. If that is the case, is that something he or she can assure you will happen? It is not uncommon for a builder to be spreading his team across several projects.

Detailed plan with interim deadlines

Sit down with your builder and draw up a detailed plan of the project with interim deadlines and the associated costs, so you can prepare for each bill as it comes. From the start you should have a list of everything you need to think about and when. Your builder should also be able to set deadlines for everything, giving you actual dates rather than words like 'soon' or 'in a few weeks'. You will need to be flexible as life doesn't always go according to plan, particularly where houses are concerned, but if deadlines are way out this needs to be addressed. Badger him/her because if they are handling multiple jobs it really will be a case of he who shouts the loudest...

Deadlines will also help you to prepare for any research or decisions that need to be made along the way, as otherwise they tend to be thrust upon you at the last minute. For some reason a lot of builders I've worked with only think about what is needed next when it's urgent. I love the interior design side of the renovation the most and it was the carrot keeping me going for months when I was also expecting a baby. I then found myself with a three week-old baby in my arms and a builder in front of me saying he needed to know the colour of paints for every room by the end of the week. He and I are no longer friends!

You would be amazed how long it can take to find the little details like the right light switch. An electrician put plastic ceiling roses and lamp holders in the middle of the ornate Victorian plaster ones in every single room because we hadn't thought about the fact we needed to get appropriate vintage metal ones. But also if you are coerced into buying in a rush you won't have the chance to make sure you are getting the best deal for your money. This plan will help your builder as well though. It's not something a lot of people like to spend the minutes doing but saves a huge amount of time and money in the long run.

Be a good client

If we want a good relationship with our builder it goes both ways. So before you go throwing your toys out of the pram, ask yourself are you being a good client?

Here's a handy checklist:

✓ Be honest with each other. If you want them to be straight with you, it's important you put all your cards on the table as well. If you're concerned about things or struggling to make decisions, tell them what's on your mind.

✓ If there's a problem flag it up early – this works both ways. If you haven't said anything about an issue, you can't then moan about it – although a decent builder will usually be on top of things. Talk to them about anything you are unsure of on the build because you both need to know where you stand.

✓ Be polite and treat them with respect. This is a business transaction, so you don't need to end up best friends, but it makes life easier if you're civil to each other.

✓ Pay the invoices on time. Obviously you don't need to pay everything up front, but if the work is being done, you should be keeping up with your side of the bargain. The final bill should be paid within a month of completion of the snagging list, but never pay until it has been completed.

Don't cut corners

Don't be cheap and don't expect your builder to be either! If you cut corners, at best it will more than likely end up costing you more to correct. Worst case is that it could make your property unsafe. Any builder worth his salt won't even entertain this option. Always remember that the builder has a duty of care to you as a client. This means that it should be as much in his/her interest as yours to do a good job.

Micro-manage!

If you employ a building company do not expect to be able to hand everything over to them and for them to get on with the job to your every specification. There are builders out there who are very capable of doing this, particularly when you pay the upper end of the scale, but don't count on it. My experience is that they are handling many projects at the same time and will never be as invested in your home as you are.

Micro-managing is not going to be welcomed, but it will certainly keep them on their toes. I think one of the things I have found incredibly frustrating is that I will tell them what I want and they ignore it and go down the easy route. By the time you notice the mistake, they are way over the deadline and all you want to do is get it finished because you're either living there amongst the detritus or you're paying rent on top of your mortgage. Plus the cost of any corrections is likely to come out of your pocket without you realising it. Therefore expect to have to project manage the project manager if you really care about the outcome, budget and time-scale. To reiterate this point I need to tell you about the time a plumber cut the down-pipe for a rain shower so that unless you were under 5'5" you would need to crouch to wash your hair. He was about 6'3" so probably did a lot of crouching while fitting it too! His response to my calm pointing out of said error was: "yeah I wondered about that as I was cutting it". Enough said.

Don't let them fob you off with jargon as well. If you don't understand, say so – it does not show weakness but rather a vested interest in YOUR property. Having said all this, there is nothing to be gained from being arrogant – particularly if you are inexperienced. It's more about being aware of what is going on so you can flag up anything alarming. If in doubt ask.

Write everything down

With one builder we started off having weekly meetings with him. He would dutifully write down everything we said and fill us with confidence. He then left his notepad behind and (because it was open...) I noticed his scribble didn't even make sense and none of the projects had been labeled. I was possibly about to get the dolphin tiles as requested by Doris down the road.

I have learned to come up with a detailed list of requests for every single room, which includes diagrams. These are added to a central folder, but also stuck to the door of the room so there can be no overlooking of vital points. When I first did this the guys actually working on the job said this was really useful to them – mainly because Mr Notepad was rarely on site and even more rarely communicated our desires to his workers. If you expect them to follow your instructions to the letter though, they do need to be 100% accurate. For example, one door on a diagram was opening the wrong way, so the electrician assumed the existing door was going to be changed, so put the light switches in the wrong place, as he was dutifully following the plan.

At the very least, any decisions or changes in the plan should be emailed. Agree with your builder that they must confirm receipt.

Don't be afraid to seek a second opinion

Although builders should be experts in their field, don't always take their word as gospel. Quite often, particularly if they have given you a job quote, as opposed to a daily rate, they will persuade you to make a decision that is easier, quicker and cheaper for them, but not always the best or most aesthetically pleasing for you. If you feel unsure about something they are trying to steer you towards or away from, speak to an independent builder who doesn't have self-serving motives. I have brought in an expert in Victorian restoration before as the builder was warning me that the ceilings might fall on my baby – yes he really did say that. It turned out that with some TLC they were perfectly sound. The irony was that the time taken to secure them was probably equal to the job of ripping down and replacing them anyway.

Be a weather forecaster!

The truth of the matter is that even the best of builders may have their heads down, rather than looking ahead. Any extra help you can give will work in your favour. If they are talking about fitting the flat roof and you know there is a frost due, you can help to avoid costly issues. It also shows you're one step ahead. I've been told countless times that the weather is the reason for them not turning up or not being able to do something. When really they're doing a job around the corner that is better paid because it's only a couple of days' work they're squeezing in. Having said that I've also been told that a dog's funeral was a reason for missing a day.

Don't be a hospital job

If you are not based at the project, make sure the builder isn't using your place as a 'hospital job'. This is where they prioritise other projects and only send tradesmen in when they're not needed elsewhere. It has happened to me and I have heard of many others going through the same. Make it clear you are keeping an eye on the project and flag any concerns as soon as you have them.

Invest in a mountain of dust-sheets
In an ideal world you will be fitting the carpet as a final step, but life isn't ideal and it may be that you could only afford the building work later down the line. There will also be some snags that need finishing off at the end. *You* will probably treat your freshly painted, carpeted house with kid gloves for a while, because, like your nerves, it will all feel a little fragile. Don't expect any tradesmen you have in to take the same care. They tend to focus on the job in hand and there will be casualties along the way unless, like a serial killer, you cover all areas yourself with dust-sheets. These don't need to be expensive. I bought a load of sheets and curtains from charity shops, which I now layer up in advance, with polythene sheets as a base.

Don't be afraid to sack 'em!
If you've followed my advice but still feel like you're banging your head against the wall it's time to give them warning that unless they pull up their socks they're out. If you're just not getting through to your builder, they aren't turning up or just simply aren't doing a good job then don't waste any more time. Line up another one and terminate the relationship. Whatever it costs to finish is what you deduct from the final bill.

Dealing with architects

It may be that on your first project you won't be doing something complicated enough to need an architect. Talk to your builder about this as they may even provide the necessary drawings themselves. If you do need planning permission you may be entering architectural territory. Local architects are usually very good at advising you on how to get planning permission and what the council is likely to want to see. They will usually oversee the whole planning procedure.

When looking for an architect you're safest going with a Royal Institute of British Architects (RIBA) qualified one. You can find more information at www.architecture.com. The advice is similar to that of employing a builder, it's still wise to have recommendations, and to make sure they are used to doing similar projects to the one you propose. Also be aware that some architects are after award winning designs! I recently wanted to build a very simple structure on a garage plot. I actually spoke to five architects in the end as most of them seemed to want to create something worthy of a Grand Designs episode! Always go for the architect who seems to listen and understand what you are after. Remember you are the client! If it's a fairly simple project, you may find an architectural technician is sufficient and more cost effective.

Allow your builder to deal with the architect or technician directly as it will help to avoid a breakdown in communication.

To do list

- Work out what you can and can't do yourself
- Enlist friends and family to help with DIY
- If necessary, ask for builder and architect recommendations from friends
- Get at least three quotes
- Check paperwork of trades people
- Set budget and deadline
- Plan works with interim deadlines
- List everything you need to choose and/or buy
- Buy dust sheets
- Put your builder and architect in touch with each other

CHAPTER 12:
Making improvements

We need to establish the general improvements that do and don't add value to a house. It's easy to get carried away and blow the budget on making it a swanky pad, but there will always be a ceiling for the price you can fetch for a place. The key recipe is to know what your future buyers are likely to want, what your property is lacking and how much you are likely to make from your improvements, so you can work out what is and isn't worth spending money on. Obviously most of this should have been part of your due diligence when buying the place, but once you have the keys it's all too easy to get carried away in all the excitement! The advice I'm giving is assuming that you are at the lower end of the market. Obviously the higher the value of the property the higher the demands of the buyer will be.

Improving the kitchen

We all know that kitchens and bathrooms are important to modern living, and invariably are what will make or break the desirability of a home. One thing people seem to misunderstand though is that this doesn't mean they should spend an extraordinary amount of money on them. Even more importantly, they don't need to be ultra-fashionable. If you are doing up your forever home, feel free to go to town. But if you are only going to live there for a short while and are looking to make money on a house, you want it to be modern, light, bright and demonstrating a clever use of space. It does not need to be expensive, particularly if the house itself is low to medium level on the market. If your property is at the upper end of the market, expectations will be greater and the margin you can make on a property is much greater, but even then you don't want to go crazy because you need to be appealing to the masses. Also it's important to make sure the kitchen style suits the period of the house – a retro cottage kitchen in a modern apartment is going to put a lot of people off!

Here are your key considerations:

Do you really need new units?
One thing worth considering is whether you actually need to put a whole new kitchen in at all. If the cupboard fronts are dated but you look inside and the carcasses are in good nick you could potentially just replace the doors and worktop, saving yourself a fortune. It may even be that you can paint the doors, depending on their style. When doing this, preparation is ultra-important. This may be the most boring and laborious of tasks, but making sure you sand to get a key, use primer and the appropriate paint will make for a better finish, but more importantly a longer lasting one – which means you won't have that laborious task again any time soon!

Kitchen colours
Going for lighter colours is really important. I can't stress this enough. It's a hard rule for me who loves nothing more than to paw over interiors magazines, easily swayed by gorgeous tones. If you think you will be there for a few years, then fine go for a daring wall colour, but anything expensive to replace needs to be sporting muted tones. White and pale grey are best, cream if you have to, but it's a little too close to 'magnolia' for my liking! The same goes for the style of cupboards and handles – the more simple the better. When you come to sell, you may not have anyone going 'wow I love those crystal doorknobs', but you also won't put anyone off. Remember the orange kitchen story that fuelled my parents' divorce…bet whoever put that in thought they were ultra-daring and modern, but they would certainly have achieved a better price without it! By the way, it may be that you can buy handles and worktop more cheaply separately than those that come with the kitchen. This is something to be discussed with your builder or supplier.

The walls also need to be neutral but it works well to have a slightly different colour to the units for differentiation. Don't forget you need to use special kitchen paint, as standard emulsion will get marked within minutes of any cooking and the associated condensation. I know it all sounds a bit bland, and it still needs to feel like your home for the time being, but there are ways to put your personality stamp on a kitchen without moving away from the strategy. I'll talk about adding temporary colour later, but the great thing about a kitchen is you have plenty of scope for accessorising. I currently have white units and dove grey walls. The yellow tea caddies, table runner, heat pads, bottles, vases, candlesticks and even a canary yellow colander give it the pick me up I need. At Christmas time it changes to a grey and red theme with ease. It's so nice to have the freedom to ring the changes in the year like that too!

Sleek, charcoal kitchens can be very cool, modern and sexy, but go darker and you're appealing to a smaller audience I'm afraid. If you're desperate to lean to the darker side, you could maybe plump for a graphite coloured worktop, to break up an otherwise white kitchen. You're still better off going for all white, or white and wood. We have often gone for oak worktops, but bear in mind they can tire quickly and you do need to oil them regularly. If you have wooden flooring and cabinets, beware of having too much wood in the room as it can start to feel like a sauna, and no one wants to think of a sweaty man crouching in the corner of their kitchen. Well most don't anyway, so once again you would be reducing the appeal!!!

If you want to have something with a little more personality, you could maybe go for a slightly patterned tile splash back. Before you finalise your choice though, do a straw poll amongst your friends and if they are divided then that's how you can expect potential buyers to be in the future! This is a good tip for anything you are choosing that will be expensive to replace before you sell, as friends and family are really great at being blunt about these things…even once they've been fitted and it's too late!

Choosing and buying a kitchen
If you are in need of a brand new kitchen, there are a few options. You can go with a builder who will have a couple of preferred kitchen providers. The quantity they buy from that company throughout the year will determine the kind of discount they can get for you. Don't forget they will cream some off the top. If you ever want to see some eye-watering (and frankly ludicrous prices) ask to see the 'invoice'. It's helpful to know that the prices in this

Kitchen before renovation

Finished kitchen

invoice are not the prices the builder pays – the provider will inflate them so they can make you feel better about what you end up paying! Remember though that the builder or kitchen supplier needs to turn some profit in order to cover the cost of correcting anything that goes wrong whilst under guarantee.

You can go to your high street store and they will usually have fitters. Bear in mind that although these fitters are used by that branch, it doesn't guarantee how good their work will be. In busy times they may be forced to take on unknown people to fulfil the workload. Going to a high street store will, however, give you the opportunity to go through a design layout with an expert. You will be amazed at how neatly they can fit all sorts into a small space. If you can get a seating area into your kitchen you are onto a winner as it becomes a sought-after kitchen/diner. Remember they are on commission so beware the 'upsell' as they entice you to buy a couple of integrated wine racks at the price of a honeymoon in the Maldives... Seriously, ask for a breakdown before deciding on any extras as they really mount up and aren't necessary in a house you will be going on to sell in the near future. Just remind yourself that in your forever home you can have a wine cellar... eyes on the prize!

Think well ahead when it comes to buying a kitchen. Have you noticed the adverts for sales at home improvement stores over bank holiday weekends? Well buy a kitchen at other times of the year and you will be paying more for the privilege. You often only need to put down a paltry deposit like £50 to secure sale prices later if you're not ready to purchase at the time (as long as you know the store has a kitchen you want). Also never be afraid to haggle as even at high street stores the price can be moveable – at the very least try to get something else thrown in.

Appliances

You will pay a hell of a lot more for built-in appliances, and it doesn't always reflect the quality and therefore longevity of that product. Now I'm in two minds about this. I think in some kitchens it's essential that white goods are hidden, and this neatness can make the kitchen appear bigger. But if there's a hall cupboard where a substantially cheaper free-standing washing machine could be kept use that. Or you could just have an open carcass for the fridge freezer, so you continue the line of the units but don't have the added cost of the doors. This will all save money. Remember if they are integrated you are most likely leaving them behind when you sell as well. This should be factored into the selling price, but you certainly won't get back what you pay for them. Even the appliances you will take with you should be bought sensibly. It's easy to go overboard with these when your money could be better spent elsewhere on features that will increase selling power. A new fridge or oven is like a new car – as soon as it's off the shelf it is losing value.

Kitchen island

Having an island in a kitchen has been popular for quite a number of years and is a trend that looks like it is here to stay. I am personally a big fan as long as they aren't squeezed in. If it can multi task as a seating area, all the better. Ideally make them mobile so you can rearrange according to needs, and this flexibility could be a strong selling point. Just think of how many times you have been to a friend's house and the position of their cutlery drawer makes no sense to you!!!

Exchange your kitchen

Did you know you can buy and sell used kitchens? You may be able to recycle the old one and put in a perfectly suitable second hand one, saving a fortune and the environment. These have sometimes come from people's homes but often from showrooms for some of the most expensive brands. So you could get a swanky one for a fraction of the price. Check out www.UsedKitchenExchange.co.uk for more details.

Practical considerations in the kitchen

Points to think about when designing your kitchen are:

- Anywhere someone is 'doing something' like a sink or an oven, they don't want to be banging their heads on units!
- Sockets need to be at least 300mm horizontally from a hob, cooker, sink or even a drainer.
- People often like to look out of a window when at the sink – but this is not essential.

- If you can get a dishwasher in, even a teeny one, it's a real plus.
- Go easy on drawers, as cupboard space is more usable and won't cost you as much, although you do need somewhere to put your cutlery and that all important 'bits and bobs' drawer!
- Under unit lighting can make for fantastic dinner party ambiance, but most future buyers will be viewing the house in daylight so won't even notice this. Save fancy extras like this for your eventual dream pad. Or for a cheaper option you can buy stick on battery-operated lights as they are hidden by the overhang.
- Bins are a real eyesore. If you can find a way to hide them fantastic, but always consider where they are going to go anyway.

There are some boring, but important, practicalities when it comes to kitchens. Make sure you are always in accordance with building regulations. Annoying as they are, they are set for a reason and it usually comes down to your safety. Even if you're moving on swiftly you don't want to have left a death trap for the next owner.

I was really adamant I didn't want an extractor hood over my hob as it would ruin the flow of the room. Next thing I know I have mould in the room that comes off the kitchen. I had an extractor fan put in and the problem disappeared! A lot of condensation is created in the kitchen, even for hopeless microwave chefs like me, so it's worth bearing in mind as it's usually much more costly to fix later than at the time.

The layout of your kitchen
If you are restructuring at all, it's worth thinking about how you might make it open plan. It may well be that a simple tap will uncover an easily removed stud wall. These days you are better off having an open plan lounge/kitchen than having a one-bum kitchen, as people hanker after a sense of light and space. This is only to be considered if it isn't at an unnecessary cost.

If you have the space, think about zoning your kitchen to include a snug area. This is particularly desirable for family house-hunters, as the luxury of their littluns having somewhere to sit comfortably whilst mum or dad make dinner is a godsend. This shouldn't be

Small kitchen before renovation

Kitchen moved and snug created

Example of kitchen extended into lean-to area

crammed in though, and shouldn't be at the expense of an eating area. It may be that even a couple of bean bags in a cosy corner give you another zone in the room and bam you have another selling point.

A lot of period terraced houses have an old fashioned lean-to crying out for modernisation. Extending into this dead space to make a decent sized kitchen can really work well. If you can do so in partnership with your neighbour, all the better, as you can share the cost and avoid boundary concerns.

Improving the bathroom

It's always very obvious when a bathroom is old and tired. So it's highly unlikely you will be able to polish one up to the spec that people expect from a recently refurbished house. Don't jump to this conclusion though and get carried away with the thought of kitting one out from scratch unnecessarily. Are there elements you could refurbish that would modernise and freshen it up? For example if the units are white and in fairly good condition, would retiling, or even just re-grouting make a difference? Does the floor just need redoing? Or perhaps an old plastic toilet seat could be replaced with a new higher quality one? There are companies that even repair the finish of old bathroom furniture, including holes. If it's avocado, with dolphin tiles, a stained toilet bowl and bubbled lino, it's time to rip it all out though I'm afraid!

When it comes to bathrooms, the same rules apply as for kitchens. Yes it's really important that it feels modern and attractive but it doesn't have to cost a fortune. I've had some eye watering quotes to kit out the smallest of bathrooms and it actually makes me really cross. Once more, I reiterate you don't want to cut corners on quality but at the same time you need to make sure that your home improvements are not going to break the budget.

Bathroom layout
When you're considering the layout think about who your target homeowner is going to be. If it's a young professional couple all they want is a decent shower and this will save you a lot of space.

If it's a family home, you really ought to squeeze a bath in. As any parent will testify, a bath is essential when you have a baby, so not having one could actually affect your footfall when coming to sell. If you're really tight for space then even a diddy bath is better than none at all, and you can get one that doubles up as a shower.

It's really important you think about layout early on. Watch out for sloping ceilings as most people want to be able to stand in a shower! I've also seen a couple of properties where they have had to put up a stud wall for a shower, because there wasn't a corner available. This can look quite cumbersome. In one case the stud wall even jutted out in front of the window, looking pretty bizarre, and reducing light. Instead you can fit a D-shaped shower, which gives you more flexibility.

His n' hers basins are really not necessary, unless you have excessive space. You're better off using the area around a basin for storage. And please please please no bidets! These are a waste of money, space and will date a bathroom.

If you haven't the software to plan out your bathroom, just cut out graph paper shapes to scale to represent the various bathroom items, so you can move them around to see how it works best. There are vital elements, like where the soil stack is, to consider though, so this is worth discussing with your builder or bathroom fitter before you actually buy the items.

Bathroom storage
Storage space is really important in a bathroom. We tend to need a lot of 'stuff' in the washroom and it can all start to feel very cluttered if out on display (unless it's a Jo Malone room spray!). So when planning your layout, think about how the spaces in between furniture can help to hide your personal bits and pieces.

Buying new bathroom furniture
Whether you order in store or online, one thing you may find is that pieces are delivered with parts missing and/or broken. That's not usually a problem because the companies I have used have been very quick to replace them. But you do want to make sure you are on top of things and checking them thoroughly as they are

Example of a well-proportioned bathroom

delivered. If you leave it to the builders they will probably not get to that until they are just about to fit them. If bits are missing or faulty this will not only stall any work, but the delayed time will most likely come out of your pocket.

Make sure that you have always ordered well in advance and that's where communication with your builder is vital. You want to know when you're going to need these items and when they will be delivered so you can make sure you're going to be around with a checklist at the ready to go through every single one. This is where I get out my clipboard and everyone finds it most amusing! Now this does require a level of organisation and dedication but if you think of it in pounds per minute and how many hundreds of pounds it will be saving you, it's definitely worthwhile. Usually once you have notified the supplier of any of the missing or broken parts they will be quick to act and you quite often get them delivered as soon as the next day. Again remember to wait until there is a sale on to order in the first place.

If it's a small bathroom you will probably need to have everything fitted to maximize the small area available. But if you have more space to play with it's worth considering having a couple of standalone items of furniture in there. This will give it a 'boutique' rather than 'off-the-shelf' feel. Also you will be able to take those items with you in the future, so your investment isn't going entirely into what will be left behind.

Bathroom tiling

When it comes to tiling, less is more – in quantity and detail. The more pattern and extra frills you have, the more likely they are to date. No matter how cute and kitsch those cacti tiles seem now, trust me they will cost you dearly when you come to sell. You don't need to tile every inch of wall space as well. Merely covering areas that are likely to come into contact with water will save you quite a bit in both materials and labour. If white tiles are just not exciting enough for you then you can get a whole rainbow of grouts now – including glitter ones! Bear in mind that going down this route is a luxury though as I would advise you to re-grout with white or grey when you come to sell.

Don't ever be tempted to cut costs by tiling over the top of existing tiles. You may find they pull away due to the sheer weight of them. The best of my bathroom transformations was a happy accident. We had to remove the pink dolphin tiles (obviously) and discovered some gorgeous rustic Victorian brickwork underneath. Suddenly there was a bathroom with character and all that was needed was a small amount of scraping, a coat of PVA and minimal tiling in the shower and above the basin.

Tiles tend to come in batches and the colours differ vastly between sets. So make sure you buy more than you need from the same batch and then keep some behind in case any crack or chip in the future.

It's important to hide all pipework as this can really ruin the finish of a bathroom. Boxed in areas can provide handy storage space as well. I've often used wainscoting for this purpose, which I think is a charming touch in a period property.

Decorating and accessorising in your bathroom
I love bathrooms. Even as a child my mum tells me whenever we went anywhere I always wanted to go into the ladies to see what it was like. I still do that now as I love to see how high-end restaurants and hotels do theirs! The thing is though you are not after an all-singing all-dancing loo! So before you go crazy and plan to install an aquarium in the shower wall (yep seen that) or diamanté encrusted taps (yep seen that too!), remember a bland bog is better than a blingy one when you come to sell in the future. Be careful not to get carried away with fashion again. You will see gold coloured taps in the celebrity interiors photos, but going for chrome that has stood the test of time is more likely to see you to your dream home sooner…in which you can have the Jacuzzi and the water wall feature because you've earned it!

Colour-wise, there is nothing safer than white, it may feel clinical, but you can break it up with carefully chosen items (not with clutter though please!). Make sure you use endurance or specialist bathroom paint for any untiled walls. Even with an extractor fan, which you must always have, there is likely to be some condensation and before you know it your freshly painted walls have gone streaky.

Bathroom with exposed brickwork

It's better to go for glass screens rather than a shower curtain as they look tired pretty quickly but are also far less appealing for future buyers (I always imagine them sticking to naked bodies yuck!).

To make a bathroom more interesting, but without putting off your eventual potential buyers, items like decorative or unusual loo roll holders, bright towels, or maybe a large ornate mirror can add character, but in a way that can be changed relatively cheaply if needs be when you come to sell. I always like to have plants in a bathroom to soften the angles and the clinical feel of having everything white. Plants often do well in bathrooms too because of the humidity. But there are some amazingly realistic faux plants on the market these days if you're lacking natural light...or green fingers!

Bathroom flooring
When it comes to flooring in a bathroom, carpet is both dated and impractical, so it's best to go for hard surfaces. Tiling can be quite cold unless you opt for underfloor heating, which I go into in the next chapter. Real wood flooring in the bathroom is also problematic. If the bathroom is above ground level and there are cracks, any water on the floor could soak through to the ceilings below. Wood is not ideal in rooms where there is a lot of moisture either, as it expands and contracts. The most cost effective solution is to go for specialist bathroom laminate flooring, which won't react in response to the changes in temperature and humidity. Be warned though that even this specialist flooring is only splash proof and won't take a constant soaking.

Relocating your bathroom
If it's really necessary to move the position of a bathroom, bear in mind that if your new spot is away from plumbing it can be quite expensive to relocate. Always ask yourself how necessary that move is. If you're gaining an extra room because of it, it's probably worth it, but if you're just swapping it's doubtful you would recoup the cost when you come to sell.

Replacing windows

If you have taken over a proper doer-upper it's likely the windows will need some attention, if not totally replacing. This could be your single most expensive cost when doing up a house. If the old ones are in good enough condition, or can come up to scratch with stripping and painting then it could save you a lot of money. Do not underestimate how long it can take to refurbish old windows though. Also if they aren't double-glazed it will affect your Energy Performance Rating, your bills and your selling power in the future!

There is always the option of getting secondary glazing, which is much cheaper than replacing the window and can actually reduce the sound even more as the gap between the panes of glass tends to be greater than on standard double glazed windows.

UPVC windows

Remember double-glazing has been around since the '70s and UPVC ones since the '80s so just because your property has them, it doesn't mean they are any good! Many have been badly fitted or yellowed with time and can really let down the kerb appeal *and* the interior look of your property. If you do get new ones, remember to shop around. There are still some dodgy double-glazing salesmen out there so do your homework. You need to make sure you're getting a decent warranty and that they are signed off by a building inspector. If you are going to do any extensions, it's worth waiting so you can get matching windows and probably at a lower price because of the higher quantity you'll be buying. If you have builders in they are likely to be able to fit them for you, but make sure they are experienced in this area and you will only get a FENSA certificate if they are registered. Any warranty will need to come from the actual manufacturer as the builder will usually only cover the labour.

Replacing sash windows

If they are old sash windows they can rattle terribly. I once rented a flat where I didn't have a single full night's sleep as a result of the windows. The old ones can be dismantled quite easily to be repaired though, along with the cords and pulleys. Most parts should be available to buy separately. You should check for any rot in the frame or sills though.

New sash windows do tend to be more expensive than typical replacement windows, but for me it's quite important you honour that style. When you put modern looking windows on an old house it really jars. If it's a listed building or in a conservation area they will usually need to be replaced like for like anyway. You can get new wooden sash windows, but they are more expensive than UPVC and you will have more upkeep, as they need to be painted every 5-8 years. They will have a draught seal and double-glazing (if allowed) though. I think this has to be a decision for you to make. If you do have original windows my heart says either repair them and add secondary glazing or invest in new wooden ones as they are more appealing than UPVC, but this will very much depend on your budget and how many windows you need to replace.

Front door

First impressions really do count and the door says a lot about a property. If it's old and decrepit your future buyers will expect the same of the whole house. But you have to live there in the meantime too and I think it has a psychological effect on you if you are greeted by a sad door every time you come home! It may be that it just needs a lick of paint and new furniture but it's not likely to offer much security if it's old. I'd go for more traditional colours like dark blue, black, red, green or grey. Pink doors may be all the rage at the time of writing this, but you will be putting off a big section of the market for the sake of being trendy. If you're adamant you want it to stand out and you will be living there for a few years you could always repaint when you come to sell, as it's not a huge job.

If the door is beyond repair this is another opportunity to improve your Energy Performance Rating as older ones tend to be pretty draughty. A door can really make a difference to the front of the house, so this is worth budgeting for. Make sure that it is up to modern security standards.

There is also the option to refurbish an old one you might pick up from a reclamation yard or from second-hand websites online. Whatever you go for, it is important to get it right and in keeping with the age and style of the house. Also get an expert to fit it as doors are notoriously hard to hang properly!

Flooring

Flooring choices I'm fairly divided on. It's quite an interesting dilemma as it is so subjective, but rarely inexpensive. Bear in mind that carpet does tend to look shabby much faster than floorboards.

Floorboards

If you're buying an older property and it's already carpeted, you may have a treat when you peel it back to find original floorboards. These may need a bit of a sand, stain and varnish, but will certainly save a small fortune and be in-keeping with the house. However, all too often plumbers and other trades people butcher floorboards making it hard to give them a new lease of life. You can replace the damaged boards but you will probably find that even after sanding and staining, the colours don't match and the repaired ones stick out like sore thumbs. On ground level you may find original floorboards quite draughty. Although this might not be something that people notice when you're selling the house it will be costly and possibly uncomfortable for you and let's not forget energy inefficient in the meantime.

If you think you can fill in the cracks think again! Trust me, as someone who has been on her hands and knees many times, for many hours, in fact days, in various properties, this is rarely successful. The wood expands and shrinks with changes of temperature and humidity so the filling just ends up falling through the cracks. If you really insist on giving it a go, your best bet is actually to use wood slithers which fit between the floorboards and behave the same way as the wood but there is still no guarantee that these won't fall through and you're back to square one.

However, you may not see a draught as a bad thing and in fact better for circulating air in the house. In that case it's relatively easy to bring the floorboards to a decent state yourself to save money. Simply hire a floor sander from a local rental shop, along with the sanding pads – make sure you have enough of these as it can be quite frustrating to run out halfway through! Start with medium to rough pads, and end with fine ones to get an even finish. Make sure you fit the pads correctly as otherwise they snap, with the most almighty bang, and before you know it you've run out of them. Always do a staining test patch somewhere discreet. It can be very disappointing how a stain

A hallway before renovation

Original Victorian floorboards after renovation

presents itself against different types and ages of wood. Very rarely does it look like it does on the tin. Don't scrimp on your finish, which will of course keep your floor looking good for longer.

Another option is to paint floorboards. I personally love this effect, but it's not for everyone. Watering down the paint to give it more of a wash is a safer bet and can really add light to an otherwise dark room or corridor. You need to make sure you prepare the wood first with a decent sand to get a key, otherwise the paint will chip and look shabby in no time.

Wood flooring or wood effect appeals to most people when you come to sell and it's a lot easier to get right than the colour and pile of carpet. The most expensive type is solid wood flooring. Engineered wood flooring is a mid to high-end price option and is basically a composite of many layers, with a top veneer of natural wood so it looks solid. It actually behaves better than solid wood as it's less sensitive to the atmosphere of the room. Depending on the thickness of the top layer you can usually refinish 2 – 6 times in the future. There are some reasonably priced laminate floorboards out there these days. Apart from the pattern repeat, which in smaller rooms you don't necessarily notice, the higher quality boards can look very authentic.

If you are a little bit handy with DIY, fitting flooring is relatively straightforward if you have the right tools, and I stress you DO have to have the appropriate tools to get a decent finish. You will find a 'how to' video on my vlog www.TheHomeGenie.com. If you think that this is beyond you, a local handyman should be able to step in. Ask for some examples of their work as I have seen some pretty bad jobs in the past. Most of the modern floorboards on the market tend to be tongue and grove or 'T&G'. These click together, which means you don't get draughty gaps and you also have some sort of underlay, which provides added proofing. So even if you lay this over the top of, let's say Victorian boards, you should find the heat efficiency improves.

Tiling
Tiling can be a little more expensive to lay but can look amazing with the right tiles and can bring alive an otherwise boring room.

Do bear in mind that you are unlikely to make the money back when you sell the house, and again tiles can be down to personal taste. Cheaper tiles can still be fairly expensive to lay and don't necessarily last or look new for long which will date a house.

Carpet

Personally I love floorboards, particularly in high-traffic areas, but I do like to have carpet in the bedroom and the lounge for comfort and warmth. It also helps to have carpets down on stairs and upper levels to reduce noise. If your carpet looks a little tired before you sell, hiring a shampooing machine can really do wonders to freshen them up. Remember though, a carpet is only as good as the underlay. So there's no point getting an expensive carpet but cutting costs on the underlay. If the colour of the original carpet is fine and it just needs freshening up, rather than replacing, new underlay and a shampoo, could save you a fair bit.

A rug made from whipped carpet to soften a lounge

When choosing carpet go for fairly light, neutral colours. If you worry about stains, a slightly darker fleck is fine. If you go for dark or vibrant colours it will make the room appear smaller and put off a number of potential buyers.

If you want to soften rooms, a rug can do wonders. I've discovered that choosing a carpet and having a piece whipped (the edges bound) can be a cheaper way of finding just the right size and colour for that room. You can then take that with you when you move so it's not a wasted cost. You may even find your local carpet shop has an offcut you can have or buy at a fraction of the cost. A rug is also a clever way to break up too much wood in a room.

Underfloor heating

So many people swear by underfloor heating, particularly in kitchens and bathrooms. Yes it does feel amazing on a cold winter's day, but can be expensive to fit, run and when it goes wrong it can be a costly upheaval to fix. It's one of those luxuries that is a bonus but won't necessarily drive someone to buy a house, and won't always add enough to the asking price to make it worthwhile financially. Check with local agents how much demand there is for properties of your size with underfloor heating before you splash out. For smaller homes though, if you're desperate for wall space, this might be your best option. You need to make sure the flooring you go for is compatible with the type of system you put in.

Radiators

Oh the radiator dilemma! Many an attractive room has been destroyed by an ugly rad. If your home is in such a state that you need to have all new plumbing, it's likely your radiators will need to be replaced as well. If you're getting rid of these, please don't just dump them in your skip, you may only make a few quid from them, but they can be recycled. Everyone is a winner as you don't fill you your skip as quickly (which costs you money), and these bulky items don't go to landfill.

If your home or style of refurb is quite modern, there are some really sleek, sexy radiators available. Don't get carried away though, as this is not something you want to blow the budget on. For period style properties it's a real shame to have standard rads, but often it's all the budget will allow. In this instance you want to disguise them. I personally really like the look of radiator cabinets, and they provide a surface for accessories. They do make a room less energy efficient though and they are not to everyone's taste. An easy way to camouflage a radiator is just to paint it the same colour as the wall. You can use standard eggshell for this. It's best to go for a water-based paint, which will stop releasing toxins (and smelling bad) more quickly than oil-based paints. You will probably find you need quite a number of coats on a new radiator, or one that hasn't been painted before. This is a job for when you can keep the windows open for a few days. You don't want to sleep in the same room until the smell subsides, and keep small children and pets away. It's a good idea to put the heating on to encourage the toxins to abate more rapidly.

If you have a period property you can get refurbished cast iron radiators, although the replica versions are far more efficient. These are pretty expensive though, so need to be a considered purchase. If it's going to be a feature in a main room, this could actually be a strong selling point and worthwhile splashing out on, particularly in higher end properties.

Fireplaces

If you're renovating a period property, it's likely to have fireplaces. Many people cover them up, but I feel that the character they add to a room can really sell a house. If you want to uncover one and need a new surround, they are often sold second-hand. Search online or at reclamation yards – but remember to haggle! Make sure you're getting a style that is in keeping with the period of the house.

If you want to use an original fireplace, you will need to get it checked by a professional to make sure the chimney is sound, otherwise you will be at risk of carbon monoxide poisoning. The chimney will also need to be swept. Wood burners are very popular these days, and can be a strong selling point. They are also more efficient than open fires. But they are quite pricey, so only worth putting in if it's a high-end property.

If you or previous owners block up a fireplace, you will need to have some kind of vent to prevent the chimney from sweating.

Lighting

Oh my goodness, where do I start? On my tours of people's homes recently, I've noticed a tendency to go for really blingy light fittings. Although this is quite popular, it is still an acquired taste. If you are looking to improve your home with a view to sell, you don't want the light fittings to stand out too much. There are a couple of reasons for this. They are a central feature so make a big difference to the interior design of the room. They can also make a room feel smaller if they are too over the top. Unless you have very high ceilings, you don't want the drop to be too low – in case Lurch is a potential buyer in the future! Classic designs are safer. Go for glass, brushed steel, or if it is a modern home perhaps a paper shade in muted tones will be appropriate.

If you don't need to rewire or replace ceilings and the like, then you may already just have light bulbs in place. This will help your budget immensely as you can buy simple pendant lights, and take them with you to the next house. Be careful not to be too cheap about these as it's always obvious. If you have a period property and you are honoring the original style, have a think about the ceiling roses. The standard plastic ones can look out of place at best and a real eyesore in some cases, particularly if they are stuck in the middle of original Victorian decorative plaster roses.

You may inherit wired lights if it was agreed in the sale, or if there are wires hanging from the ceiling, but you need to make sure there is an earth wire if you replace plastic roses with metal ones. The same goes for wall lights. You can get an electrician to replace these so you can fit the pendant lights I mentioned earlier.

I do actually think that light switches are worth replacing if they are just standard plastic ones. It doesn't cost very much but can really modernise a house. You don't need to go for really expensive bespoke ones, but make sure they are good quality. If you are rewiring the place it's something to think about and to purchase early on as your electrician will probably just fit standard plastic ones otherwise and charge you for it.

Spotlights can be a great way to get light into the corners of the room, but unless you are starting from scratch it's not worth the expense of having these put in if there's a traditional light in place. Side lamps can easily give you the desired effect.

Improving internal doors

Internal doors can be a big deal for some people while others don't give them a second thought. Of course everyone would love to have solid wooden doors, but it will cost you a small fortune to replace all of them, so is rarely worth it, unless you are at the upper end of the market. This is something for you to decide based on the overall cost of your property (and the state of the current doors). Sometimes just a lick of paint and new handles will mean they don't stand out as much. If they have decades of paint on them you could save yourself some money by having them dipped and stripped back to the wood. If they're what I call 'angry' doors (really cheap and nasty with dents all over the place where people have kicked them during an argument!) then you have to bite the bullet. But don't go crazy with top of the market replacements because although it will improve the overall impression, you are unlikely to get the cost back when you sell the house.

CHAPTER 13:
Decorating and interiors

Decorating your home

Now we get to my favourite bit – how to make a house a home. I know this book has been very much about improving your home, with one eye on being able to sell it in the future. That *is* very important. It's the whole reason I am writing this book, to help you get on and move up the ladder like I have, so you can have the ideal home one day. But life is short and your home space is massively important to your mood, motivation and general wellbeing.

It may be that you are one of life's energy balls and will be looking to move up very soon after improving your first place, in which case you will just dive straight in with decorating to sell. In this instance, non-experimental, non-risky, muted and sophisticated are the words you should have in mind. For those of you who think that a few years may pass before you move up to the next abode, you want and need this to feel like home. You may even feel like you need a break after all your hard work and to actually enjoy the home you have for a while. So I have some tricks up my sleeve for creating that homely space without too much expense, but in a way that shouldn't hinder you selling your home next time around.

What I will say is make sure you have a plan in place. Set a deadline for when that next move will be. It's amazing how easily time can fly and before you know it circumstances change and your property climbing strategy flies out of the window. If children are on the cards, you may want to make that move sooner rather than later. If you already have kids you may want to leave it a bit longer and enjoy your time with them during those special early years. Just bear in mind that location becomes more crucial as they grow up and schooling takes over your life.

Wall colour

We are going safe on the walls or 'greige' you might say! Trust me I love the dramatic, inky colours and even the pastels in fashion at the moment, but not everybody does. If someone wants to paint a room a darker or more vibrant colour they will do so when they move in. The fact you have provided them with a blank canvas just makes this easier. White, pale grey and off-white has the effect of making a room seem bigger, lighter and therefore brighter.

The problem with other colours is they can tend to be a bit like Marmite. One person loves them, but another detests them. When I was talking at the Ideal Home Show I did an experiment, which clearly demonstrated this point. I put up images of different colours and asked people to raise their hands if they liked them. Some members of the audience vigorously waved with a big smile on their faces, whilst others grimaced and crossed their arms as the different colours flashed up on the screen. The trouble with colour is that it is divisive and you don't want to cut down your chances of getting the best price for your house in the future. Nor do you want to go to the time and expense of decorating now, and then redecorating when you come to sell. Not everyone wants a neutrally coloured home but if the colour is too provocative it turns potential buyers off the whole property. So when you strip your home of all colourful accessories when you come to sell, these muted tones will appeal to the majority of people.

Now the good news is that it is very easy to still inject colour into a room and put your stamp on it temporarily with strategic furnishings and accessories. So you *can* make it your own for the time you are there. Plus you can take these with you when you move so the cost is only a one-off.

Guide to painting and decorating

As I said earlier, the more you can do yourself, the quicker you will move up that ladder. Painting your walls is a way to really cut costs and can be incredibly satisfying. Don't be lulled into the false sense of security that anybody can do it though. It takes a lot of preparation, care, attention and the appropriate tools and paint to get it right. I still think that if you are going to do any DIY it's a good place to start. So I thought I would arm (because you will have strong arms by the end of this) you with all the tips I have learned along the way.

Removing wallpaper

If you think you could get away with keeping woodchip paper, think again. This is an immediate turn-off when you are trying to sell and it dates the property, no matter what else you do. It can be hard work, particularly as there are usually further layers underneath. Use a steamer and very sharp scrapers. The ones with replaceable blades are your best bet. I can't stress enough though, before you go to all this effort, if you notice the plaster underneath is in a bad state give up fairly early on as you will probably need to rip it out and replace with new plasterboard anyway. Don't waste days on unnecessary scraping, as take it from me, it is heart-breaking! By the same token, if wallpaper is in good condition, but you just don't like the colour or pattern, you can always use a product like Zinsser Wallpaper Cover-Up to paint over it and save yourself a lot of time and trouble.

Testers

Never be tempted to skip the colour testing stage. The little colour cards are great, but they really won't give you a precise enough guide to the final tone in that room. You may baulk at the price of a tester pot, considering how little paint you will use from it, but trust me it will be worth it. I made this mistake once. I thought it was a pleasant grey on the card, but came home to find my decorator scratching his head saying 'I hope your husband is happy with this' as he stood in my freshly painted pink kitchen. Suffice to say it needed repainting…after I'd tested out further paints! So when you get your testers make sure you try them on different walls and you see them in different lights, as the colour can change dramatically depending on the time of day.

One mistake many people make is to brush the tester paint on thickly. When you come to do your walls, it's likely you will use a roller, which gives a totally different result. It can be a real pain to

A yellow bedroom before renovation

Bedroom during renovation with door knocked through to bathroom

Bedroom after renovation in muted tones

get a smooth finish over the top of this splodge, and may require you to re-prep the wall. Dulux actually do a tester roller now so you can see the paint more realistically and it's easier to get a neater finish later. If you're ever tempted to use up the rest of a tester pot on the wall, don't bother. It's quite often made of a lesser quality paint so it will fade faster than the proper pots.

Don't forget you aren't restricted to the standard colours on offer by the main brands. I often find a wallpaper I like and then go for a colour match, a service most high street DIY stores offer. This can also be done to achieve colours similar to the very expensive brands to save money…but I didn't tell you that!

Finish

Painting your walls isn't just about the colour. The finish makes a huge difference to the overall effect. These days most people want a matt effect, so everyone reaches for the standard emulsion on walls. The problem with emulsion is it tends to mark very quickly. It is money well spent to go for an endurance paint which will not mark as readily, is easier to clean and do touch ups on, is less likely to show condensation markings, and will look fresher for longer. It also seems to take longer to fade, and it's less likely you will have to repaint before you sell, so should save you money in the long run. The ultimate is to go for eggshell on the walls, but that is quite a bit more expensive so needs to be considered carefully according to budget. There is a very slight sheen with endurance paint, but not so much that it ruins the end effect, but you will need to make sure the walls are well prepared as it tends to highlight any imperfections.

Woodwork

Think about your woodwork and what colour that will be. With the strategy of this book in mind, going for white makes most sense. I always opt for eggshell as it gives the least sheen – gloss is very outdated. Just beware that white isn't white. By that I mean if you use different 'white' paints they are unlikely to match so stick with the same brand. I'd also go for water-based (acrylic) paint as the fumes aren't as heady, they don't yellow over time like oil and you don't have to wait as long for each coat to dry, so you get the job done more quickly. Oil-based paints are more durable, but I still think acrylic is best if you are doing the job yourself.

Make sure you prep woodwork thoroughly, particularly if the original paint is old and flaking. Trust me it's just not worth skimping on this task as you will end up with a shoddy finish at best. At worst your new coat will be peeling within weeks of your hard work. Sometimes sanding for a key is simply not enough and it takes a bit more elbow grease to actually strip away old layers of paint.

Ceilings

If you are following my advice of using muted tones, you also don't want to go crazy with ceiling colour. White works with all softer shades, but there's nothing to say you couldn't go for the same colour on the ceilings and walls. Always paint the ceilings first to avoid splattering your freshly painted walls. A great tip is to use a shower cap to keep the paint spray out of your hair. Hey I never said this was glamorous work! Remember to seal any cracks first. If these are severe, you might want to get an expert in to check they are sound and won't fall down any time soon.

By the way, if there is 80's style artexing I would seriously consider having this skimmed smooth (plastered over). It may be an annoying extra cost you want to avoid but the potential buyers of the future who want to move in and do nothing, will not want to have to sort out the ceilings. Like the woodchip paper, artexed ceilings would spoil the overall impression of the refurb and therefore affect your ability to sell or sell at the price you're aiming for.

Choosing paint brands

Don't be cheap. I'll say that a little louder, DON'T BE CHEAP! Lower cost paint is likely to need more coats, mark the minute you breathe on it, and fade before you even have your shoes off at the front door. By the same token you don't need to go for the really high-end brands. Remember, we have a budget here and aren't looking to impress our mates. It's worth choosing your paint early on so you can see if there are any sales, which can save you money with a large percentage off.

Safer paints

Long gone are the days of lead-based paints in this country, but there are still concerns about the level of toxins in today's products. If there are sensitivities in your family this has to be a consideration, but either way it's worth doing your research so you are well informed. If you have children in the house, you might want to consider VOC free paint – this stands for volatile organic compounds, in case you were wondering. These do tend to be a bit more pricey but worth it for the health and safety of our littluns – particularly in nurseries or children's bedrooms.

Brushes

Oh how I love paintbrushes. Seriously, I just love them. The difference between a good and a bad brush is like comparing chalk with cheese – as is the finish you achieve. If you are using water-based paints, synthetic bristles tend to be the best as they don't absorb the water and leave track marks. Natural bristles are better for oil-based paint. You can also get combination brushes, but I'd stick with one or the other. Don't go for cheap brushes. I'll say that a bit louder, DON'T GO FOR CHEAP BRUSHES! Think of this, you stand back to admire your hard work and notice you have bristles stuck to your glorious artwork – yep that's what happens. You also don't tend to get as smooth a finish with low-cost products. If you are going to be doing fiddly bits, and/or hard to reach areas, an angled brush will be your friend.

Painting can be tiring work. By the end of a day of decorating you will be exhausted and reaching for a glass of wine (if you didn't start earlier in the afternoon). No matter how tired you are, make sure you thoroughly clean those brushes. If using water-based paint then warm soapy water is best. You will need to use your fingers to release the paint from in between the bristles, but if you want to eat your dinner first then you can soak them. It's worth using a paintbrush tub, which will hold the brush in place. If you soak the whole brush in water it is likely to destroy the glue that holds the bristles in place and rusts the metal band. For oil-based paint you will need to use white spirit (hate that stuff and it's another reason I don't like using oil-based paints).

When taking a break in between coats you can just wrap the paintbrush in cling film or a plastic bag, to prevent the air getting to it. You wouldn't want to do this overnight as it's hard to make it airtight and if the paint dries out you will spread flaky bits all over your walls the next day.

Paint pot tips

You know that tin of paint that won't close any more because of the build up? This is totally unnecessary and a waste of money as the paint goes off more quickly. Transfer a little of the paint to a kettle (a plastic pot) and you will reduce the amount of air that gets into the paint tin. A kettle is usually easier to hold as well. Another tip is to put an elastic band over the tin or kettle to scrape off excess paint from your brush. This prevents a build up on the side and also means you are less likely to get dried up bits from the edge onto your brush, which then get transferred onto the wall – unless you like the textured effect!!!

Paint rollers

For larger areas you would be crazy not to use a paint roller. It covers a larger surface area more quickly and easily, and if you use an extender you may not even need to go up a ladder to do most of the wall. Use a foam roller for wood paint and a slightly longer pile (more fluffy) for emulsion. You also need a tray for these, which must be cleaned as thoroughly as the brushes. You can get disposable paint tray covers but these are obviously not very good for the environment and frankly a lazy option!

Preparing the room

Sooooo boring and unfulfilling, but soooo necessary. First of all cover EVERYTHING. Paint has this very weird way of finding it's way through to your brand new carpet (although of course you paint the walls before you lay the carpet dur!). My tried and tested trick is to use old bed sheets, or ones from charity shops on top of polythene sheets. Cotton sheets are not enough alone as the paint soaks through, but do a good job of weighing the plastic down. This way you can reuse the plastic and bung the bedding sheets in the washing machine. For carpets you can use what is essentially sticky back plastic, but I have just never got on too well with this stuff and seem to get in a right pickle with it sticking to the wrong places. I also don't like using things I have to throw away. Many people swear by it though, so feel free to give it a whirl if it appeals. It's important to have plenty of ventilation during and after painting a room. It can also be hot work decorating so have a window open no matter the time of year.

Taping

It's really worth taking the time to apply masking tape around borders and below the skirting board. Use low tack tape to avoid peeling off paint from underneath. Masking tape is not a silver bullet though and doesn't mean you can just splosh the paint on over the top as it will often still seep through or leak around the edges. I have spent many hours and even days on my hands and knees removing paint, even to the point of having to sand, restain and varnish floorboards because a sloppy decorator didn't seem to care where the paint went.

Preparing the walls

So I am assuming that any wallpaper has been removed, if necessary. Arms ache much?! Well you need to make sure that the wall is properly cleaned and any residue has been removed. Just using warm soapy water will do, but you really want to make sure all dust, cobwebs and debris are cleared before you paint. You also need to fill dents, holes and any cracks (as long as they aren't major, in which case they need further investigation). Just using quick-dry ready-mix filler and a flat knife will do. An expired credit card to scrape off the excess works better than any tool I've come across. Once it's dried you may need to finely sand, but it's better to get it as smooth as possible when wet. If the surface is in too bad a state you might want to get a plasterer in just to skim (apply a thin layer of plaster) to give you a fresh start. This is quite a skilled job, so usually worth splashing out on someone who knows what they're doing. It makes sense for them to do a few rooms at a time because they will probably charge a day rate anyway.

Whether you are cleaning or replastering walls, it is essential they are completely dry before painting – do not be tempted to rush this. It can take a week or so for plaster to dry thoroughly.

Priming

You don't *have* to use a primer (base coat) on the walls, but it is a good idea. If you tint the primer with your final colour you should find you need fewer coats. If you're painting a light colour over darker walls, which tend to need more coats, adding a bit of a tint to the primer will definitely help. On recently plastered walls you definitely need a base coat of watered down basic emulsion otherwise the plaster absorbs the moisture, with the result of cracking paint. Make sure the emulsion doesn't have vinyl in it. Any initial coat still needs to be done neatly as it is likely to affect the final result.

Mixing the paint

Sounds obvious but you would be surprised by how many people skip this bit! Give the tin a good shake and then use a mixing stick to stir thoroughly. If you don't bother, you are unlikely to get a consistent colour and finish. Metal mixing sticks that double up as a paint tin opener are brilliant as they don't destroy the lids as well.

Cutting in

Start by 'cutting in', which is essentially brushing on a 7cm line of paint around borders and corners where the roller won't reach. You can get a specific trim brush for this, which is definitely worth investing in. It's a good idea to do a section at a time so the paint doesn't completely dry before you use the roller. This way you can blend it by feathering in to avoid tidemarks. Dip your brush in water first so as not to overload it, and then remove excess on a rag to avoid dripping. Start at corners and work your way out. Always go from top to bottom so you can correct any drips as you go.

Roller painting

Make sure you don't overload the roller, and remove any excess on the grooves of the tray. When you apply the roller to the wall, do so in the shape of a 'W', and then fill in the rest, which should give you an even finish. Work quickly and try not to go over bits that have already dried, otherwise you will see darker areas emerging. Remember that the direction of the roller you finish on will give you a different result. When you roll up it opens the pile, and a downward motion closes it, so you want to end with the latter for

Example of a subtly wallpapered chimney breast

a smoother finish. WAIT until it is completely dry before applying further coats. Patience is a painter's virtue! At the end, go over any trims that need it – and don't forgot sockets and light switches. Remove the tape before it is totally dry so that it doesn't damage the paint around it.

Job done!

Make sure you keep a note of all the colours you have used for future reference. It's also a good idea to save any leftover paint in small pots for touch ups – for this you use a small roller. Be warned the paint does tend to go off after a time.

Wallpaper

The feature wall has been a trend for quite a while, but is starting to wane. The minute you introduce a pattern to a room you are dividing your audience. It's also much easier to refresh painted walls when you come to sell than it is to remove marks and scuffs from wallpaper. If you just can't help yourself then keep it to a minimum with subtle patterns and colours. If you're only papering a small space, you might be able to benefit from batch-end rolls of paper in the sales. Never try to mix batches though as the colours will differ markedly. Many people put wallpaper on the chimneybreast. This actually makes a room feel smaller, but offers a cosy effect for bedrooms. Conversely, patterned paper on the recesses either side of the fireplace gives the illusion of a larger room.

Putting up wallpaper is not as easy as you think. Well at least getting a good result is not as easy as you think, so it's worth enlisting help. There is nothing worse than seeing bubbles and shoddy joins. A tip I give to renters is to use the temporary/removable wallpaper, which is also a good idea if you don't want to redecorate when you sell. This should peel away without damaging the wall when the time comes to put the house on the market, or you have simply grown tired of the pattern. This kind of wall art is particularly useful in children's rooms, as they tend to grow out of styles as rapidly as their shoes.

Example of peel-away wall stickers used in a nursery

How to create a colour scheme

Now we have our neutral background we can set about personalising with colours that will make it feel like home to us. This is achieved by accessorising in a more temporary way. The trick is to create a palette we can strip back when we come to sell, or even change when we grow tired of it. I'll go into the 'how' later, but for now let's just choose the colours.

The simplest way to put together a colour scheme is to imagine it in three parts. You have your base colour – about 50-60%, which is most likely your walls and floors. Your theme colour makes up about 30-40% of the room (and you might want different tints, tones and shades of this). Your accent colour contributes about 5-15%. Some call this your 'pop' colour. To give you an example, the walls in my lounge are a stone colour. I then have teal drapes, teal/turquoise artwork and vases. My accent colour is orange/gold, which is represented by a couple of cushions, a lampshade and a piece of artwork. Funnily enough I really disliked orange and gold until about a year ago and now love them. So we are not only divided on colour as individuals, but we also change our minds, which is why we have to go safe on the walls, but can be more adventurous with the embellishments.

Colour psychology

Once you have a framework for your scheme you need to come up with colours to fill it. Well the mood of the room is a really important factor and if you pick the wrong colours it may never feel quite right. If you think about some common phrases like 'feeling blue', 'tickled pink', 'seeing red' it illustrates how evocative colour is, but also how it can shape your mood when it comes to interiors.

When I am home coaching clients we identify what their main goal is in their lives currently and we shape their house to support it. That doesn't mean the whole house is going to be one colour to motivate them though. As human beings we are more complicated than that and have different needs in different rooms. So the first step is to ask 'how do I need to feel in this room?

Lounge before renovation

Lounge after renovation with colour scheme of teal and orange

Let me give you some personal examples. In my bedroom I need to feel relaxed when I go to bed, but raring to go when I get up in the morning. In my kitchen I don't want to be too encouraged to eat as we are already big eaters in this house! My snug is where my toddler Bonnie keeps all her toys so I don't want the decor to compete with the mountain of brightly coloured plastic she seems to accumulate. Meanwhile the lounge is our grown-up space where we need to relax, but I also go there to think and even work sometimes. Identify which mood you need to evoke in each room and then look at all colours to see which will do the trick for you.

Here are some notes to help you, but bear in mind that different colours – and tones, tints and shades – will affect people in different ways because of memories and general conditioning in our lifestyles and cultures:

Red is a hot colour and speaks of energy, excitement and stimulation – including sexual. It can, however, make some angry or stressed. So if you have trouble sleeping you wouldn't want this in your bedroom. If you want to improve your sex life though it might be just the ticket!

Pink, which is obviously a tint of red, makes some think of warmth, tranquility and even sexuality. It can also be claustrophobic for others, or a sign of weakness. It gives some a sense of emasculation, whereas others see it as a feisty colour. If you love it but your partner hates it, there are ways of making it more palatable, like incorporating black or dark green.

Yellow can be very emotional – in either direction. It is often seen as optimistic and creative. But it can cause anxiety. The effect you get from using yellow in a room can very much change depending on the colours you combine it with.

Green is surprisingly controversial. For many it is a very positive, harmonious and balanced colour. It is reminiscent of peaceful nature, rest and recuperation. It can promote growth and personal development. But it bores many as well and can be depleting. Don't forget that when you put plants in a room (which for me is a must) green has to be taken into account as a colour in your scheme.

Blue is often seen as a colour of calm and logical thinking so can help with reflection and communication. But it is one of the coldest colours, so to more emotional people seems aloof and even depressing! If you need calming down, but want more emotion in a room, then make sure you really go for contrasting accent colours to lift the blue. If your goal is to lose weight, blue is a good colour to use in the kitchen as it can suppress the appetite – after all, when is food blue in its natural state?

Violet is an interesting one as it is associated with vision and truth, but also luxury and opulence, which some might say are opposites. It's a colour to be used in small doses as it does tend to look gaudy when it dominates a scheme. It can be a power colour though, so if you're looking to build a business, confidence or are just into personal development violet can be a strong force in an appropriate space.

Orange is often perceived as a healthy colour (think vitamin C) but also fun. It provides comfort, warmth and passion. But it can also cause frustration and is considered by many to be an immature colour. I think it works well as a pop colour to lift a colder, darker base.

Black, although not actually a colour, can add substance to a room when used in the right way. It can make subtle schemes more dramatic and glamourous, and brighter schemes more sophisticated. Used too much though it can become oppressive.

This is obviously not a comprehensive guide to colour. Frankly a lot of that is merely speculative because at the end of the day you need to decide how colour makes *you* and the people you share your house with feel. I just wanted to get you thinking about your own perception of colour. As long as you are following my guide of being able to strip it all to muted tones when you come to sell, it is only *your* emotional connection that should matter. So many people decorate their homes according to what they think will impress others or satisfy the latest fashion, but it will never quite sit right with you if that is your only inspiration.

Another reason for being able to easily and affordably change the colour schemes of rooms is that needs and tastes can change overnight. To give you a very personal example of this, when my husband and I were trying for a baby I was taking my journalism exams whilst also working very long and anti-social hours. To say I was stressed was an understatement. I became quite obsessive about things and found it difficult to switch off. We struggled (sounds romantic eh?!) for a while to no avail. I was coaching somebody else one day when things finally clicked. I was talking the talk but not walking the walk when it came to my home environment. For one thing I felt I needed a change, but another was to make sure I had plenty of relaxing schemes around my home. I'm not going to try and say this got me pregnant – think something else went on there – but it certainly helped to calm this stress ball down!

Adversely after having my beautiful little girl I suffered from postnatal depression sadly. It was like I was seeing life through grey-tinted spectacles and my décor wasn't helping. Once I finally acknowledged this I turned to my old friend colour again and brightened up the place with pinks, yellows and oranges. It really did lift my spirits and complemented the other therapies I used like CBT to nurse me back to health. So work out where you are in your life right now, and what your mood requirements are for each room. Do you need motivation, passion, relaxation, balance, excitement, focus? Identify this and then explore which colours satisfy these needs. Houzz.co.uk and Pinterest.co.uk are great sources for this kind of research where you can actually see potential colours in place in the appropriate rooms.

Guide to the colour wheel

Now you have an idea of the colours you need in your life, the colour wheel is a great tool for putting them together as a scheme. It's worth getting one of these and they only cost a few pounds to buy online.

Here is the colour wheel explained:

Primary, secondary and tertiary colours
If you have a look at the backside of the wheel you will see your hues around the outer edge. Let's start with the primary colours

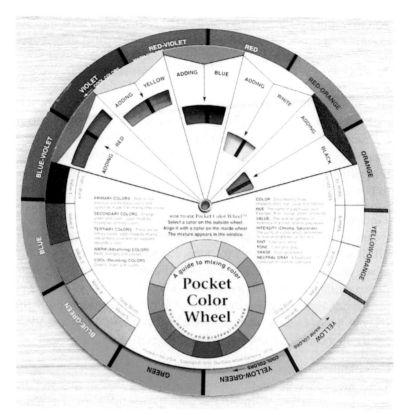

One side of the Colour Wheel

red, yellow and blue. Your secondary colours, green, orange and violet are what you get when you mix two of the primaries together. The ones in between are your tertiary colours – so red-orange, yellow-orange, yellow-green, blue-green, blue-violet and red-violet. Just seeing these set out on the colour wheel can help you when organising and choosing schemes. But there's more!

Warm and cold colours

It's worth bearing in mind that you have a cold half and a warm half to the colour wheel. When you're putting together a scheme for a room, you might want to consider this according to the mood you're trying to evoke. It may be that the room feels a little cool, for example, so needs a colour from the warm side to heat things up.

Analogous

If you're a little nervous about using colour, you might want to stick to an analogous scheme. This is where you use colours next to each other on the wheel, like green, blue-green and yellow-green. It's more reflective of what you find in nature. You want to use at least two of these colours, but no more than five, otherwise you lose the harmony. This is a safe way to use colour, but you might want to live a little once you've dipped your toe in!

Tints, tones and shades

When you mix a hue with white it gives you a tint of that colour. Mix it with grey and you get the tone. The shade is what you achieve when you mix it with black. The wheel indicates the end result of these combinations if you look down towards the centre. If you just use the tint, tone and shade of a colour it's known as a monochromatic scheme. This can look really fantastic, but you might want to add a contrasting colour for interest, which brings me to....

Complementary colours

Trust me, you will thank me for introducing you to this section! It's when you start experimenting with the complement of a colour you get the 'wow' factor. A colour's 'complement' is opposite it on the wheel. Think yellow and violet or red-orange and blue-green. Put these together and what have you got? A real pop of colour (bibbidi-bobbidi-boo!!!).

Split complementary

You can also get an awesome effect with a split complementary scheme. This is where you mix the key colour with the two either side of its complement. For example orange with blue-green and blue-violet.

Triad and tetrad

A triad includes three evenly spaced colours on the wheel, like red, yellow and blue. A tetrad has four evenly spaced colours on the wheel. These are bold uses of colour, but if you work with tints, tones and shades of the pure colours you can find more harmony.

There is more to learn but this is a good start for beginners. So now you know how to use a colour wheel, go forth and experiment. Although remember rules are there to be broken – it just boosts your confidence to know them in the first place!!!

Mood boards

Now you have a rough idea of the colours you want to incorporate into your home it's a good (and fun) idea to put together a mood board or two. This is especially true if you are going out of your comfort zone a little. If a partner is struggling to see your vision, a board can also help him or her to understand where you're coming from. I ruddy love putting together a mood board, it seriously is a good night in for me these days (boy when did my Friday nights come to this?!). But it's important you really let loose rather than be too prescriptive. It's only this way you can truly experiment and achieve something amazing.

Start with a large blank board so you have plenty of space to go crazy with ideas. I tend to go for foam boards from art shops. Don't feel you need to stick to the parameters – bits jutting out are perfectly fine, come on live a little! I use a mixture of printouts from the Internet, magazines, brochures and photos I've taken. You need to fill the background with your main chosen colour. Unless white is featuring in your scheme, you don't want to have any showing. So even if your walls are to be grey, then paint your board in that colour so you get a true representation of what will be the end result.

If you're not too set in your ways, your board will guide you on colour. If others creep in, it may lead you in a different direction or reinforce your original choices. It's important to remember that this exercise is not about making decisions on exact colours, fabrics and patterns yet, it's more about getting the mood of the room right. So you don't need to be too prescriptive. Do pay attention to the ratio of colours. You want to get a feel for how much of your pop colour you're after, for example – too much of this and it would change the whole look. You may find though that adding more of a complementary colour actually looks awesome so it's an

A mood board

opportunity to experiment. Adding different tones will help you to make the final decision. I like including scenes of my chosen colour in nature where they're most harmonious.

Remember to include different textures too, so fabric should definitely feature. If there are textures you're keen on having in the room it's important to include these either in actuality or in image. I find myself stealing things all over the place because I'm quite tactile so if I come across something that appeals to me…and there's a loose thread, it's going on the board!

Feel free to change your mind as you go. I only use sticky tack so I can remove, add and rearrange accordingly. Trust me I change my mind A LOT! Don't be too exacting on how you place items on your board as well – remember this is a creative dump, so anything goes!

My rooms always have plants and flowers so I make sure these are included. They don't *have* to be real, but I did include a piece of moss I fell in love with once. It's also worth thinking about the plants you will have in a room because different coloured leaves will have a different effect on the other colours in the scheme. Remember you need to acknowledge the woods and metals you're having too as they will impact the overall look, feel and sound of the space – yeah really!

Furnishing your home

Furnishing your home can be an expensive business. In my experience what works in one house doesn't in another so it pays to leave extravagant furniture until you reach your forever home. For years I only bought second-hand furniture and it has saved a fortune, which I was then able to invest in property. Many people hate the idea of buying second-hand, but it really will save you thousands of pounds. My current kitchen and garden tables were being thrown out by someone, so I got them for free and saved them going to landfill. Even now I buy most of my furniture for next-to-nothing and upcycle if necessary.

It's never been easier to buy second-hand as a simple Internet search will find your local outlets. Here's where to look:

Kitchen before renovation

Completed kitchen with upcycled second-hand furniture in light colours

Dining room before renovation

Dining room after renovation, with upcycled second-hand furniture

- Preloved.co.uk
- Gumtree.com
- Ebay.co.uk
- Freecyle.org
- Charity furniture shops (British Heart Foundation have a number of large stores – go to bhf.org.uk to find your local one)
- Yell.com
- Freeads.co.uk
- Reclamation yards (always haggle as they can be more pricey!)
- Furniture auctions (although items usually cost more)
- House clearances

It's really important that the colour of your furniture is considered in the scheme of the room. Also be wary of having dark furniture or too much wood, particularly where you have wooden floorboards. I often use chalk paint, which needs minimum prep, to personalise and lighten darker or outdated pieces. Check out my numerous guides at www.TheHomeGenie.com

When it comes to built-in cupboards and wardrobes, if smaller rooms are crying out for storage space they may be worth installing. But remember that this will be money going into the house you are unlikely to get back when you sell. Also some built-in furniture can be outdated and off-putting (like the units above beds eurgh!), whereas simple cupboards either side of a chimney-breast are less controversial. If the property you buy has built in units and they feel dated, think about painting them or simply replacing the doors. If you do remove them unnecessarily you may be opening a can of worms as the walls behind may not be in good nick.

Window dressing

Curtains and blinds can also be pretty costly. If you plump for curtains and manage to get the right size ready-made this will be your best bet. Be careful they don't look cheap, and don't skimp on the width as you want them to look quite full. I also think it is important that they puddle by at least 15cm as they will look richer, more voluminous and also it is easier to use them again in a future home as you have extra length to play with. I think that when they

Relaxed swags, with curtains puddling on floor

measure exactly to the floor (which is hard to do anyway) they tend to look like trousers that are too short!

If you have very long or wide windows you may struggle to find appropriately sized curtains. In this instance you will have to either make them (a little tricky to do well if you are inexperienced) or have them made. You can either go to a local seamstress, some large home stores provide this service, or there are online companies as well. It's worth shopping around and don't skimp on lining as it will affect the look of them and can cheapen a room. I always go for blackout lining in a bedroom. Even in the grandest of buildings you don't need to go for the whole swags and tails effect. For a start it will cost a great deal more, but is also an acquired taste and can easily look dated.

Make sure you know the type and quality of the walls you're attaching the curtain poles to. Vigorous pulling of curtains day in day out can take their toll and before you know it the curtains are falling down and taking half of the wall with them.

Roller blinds can be a little less expensive, but you are more likely to leave these with the property. Go for plain, modern and simple – so future buyers don't really form an opinion either way about them.

Wooden blinds can look really good in the right property, but again you want to shop around. If you're not going to be there for long there really is no need to go for the most expensive set on the market considering you are likely to leave these behind. Be careful though because cheap blinds are infamous for breaking quickly.

Do I need to tell you not to go for net curtains? Nah. But actually in rooms where you don't need privacy, some plain, floaty voile can be both cost effective and attractive.

Accessorising

This is the fun part, and is best done bit by bit over time. An easy way to add colour to a room is through strategic accessorising. Cushions, artwork, frames, vases, and even painted furniture will help to fulfill your scheme. Less is generally more which is why I say to do it over time so you can assess the impact on the room as you add each piece.

Again you can save yourself a great deal of money by buying second hand and upcycling. All the vases in my lounge I have spray-painted, the tables I have modernized and coloured with chalk paint. Even the picture frames and mirror I have painted numerous times according to the colours I needed in the room. I often make my own cushions too out of old shirts. You don't even need a sewing machine and it takes very little time as the buttons are in place before you even start! You will find video guides to all these crafts at www.TheHomeGenie.com.

Your colour scheme needs to be represented at all levels, so what you have on your walls is really important. Don't clutter them though as this will make rooms feel smaller. When it comes to hanging anything you want to be a little cautious. If you have plasterboard walls you will need specific fixings, unless you have super-strength plasterboard. If you haven't replaced the plaster on an older property it's likely to be a little frail. You can get fixings for hanging items where you stick them on and then they have a system similar to Velcro to attach them. You can then remove the fixing without damaging the wall later on.

I think a room without a mirror is like a garden without flowers (ooh mirrors in the garden can also be really lush actually!). They immediately provide a focal point. If placed opposite a window they can bring light into darker sides of a room and also make the room feel bigger. I say go large on mirrors though, as you can get away with them being pretty big, but if they're too small for the room it just looks odd. Make sure the frame is appropriate for the style of the room and house as well. I love big ornate frames in period houses, but they can sometimes look a little gaudy in new builds.

CHAPTER 14:
Other improvements

Improving the exterior

Curb appeal is so important when you're selling a house. So it doesn't make sense to primp out the interiors but leave the exterior looking like a dump.

Driveway

Depending on the area, having a driveway can be like gold dust. If it's near a train station or high street it might be worth seeing if you can create one out of a front garden. If parking on the street is a cinch then this is only a wise way to spend the budget if you know the demand is there. You do want a tidy, front patch though, so if there are broken slabs on a pathway to the front door, or a drive with potholes, it all needs to be fixed.

Roof

If the roof needs care and attention you should hopefully have known this before you bought the place. This is not something to take lightly because even if it doesn't look like a problem, any issues will cause bigger ones down below. Correcting damp, particularly after you've just renovated, will be costly and a mistake you won't make twice. Best not to make it at all. If you're handy it may be something you can fix yourself, but otherwise get someone in who knows what they're doing.

External walls

Cracking render can also let in damp and needs to be fixed and then probably painted. If the pointing (cement between the brick) is crumbling it will need redoing as well. If the paintwork is just a bit tired this may be something you can do at a later stage when you've saved up so it's fresh for when you come to sell. That can be a strong selling point as potential buyers will appreciate they don't need to get it done in the near future. There are new types of compound surfacing you can get that colours the exterior, but also lasts a lot longer. It's pretty pricey though and probably not worth the cost if you're not staying for long, but worth investing in for the forever home.

If you have cladding, make sure it's not rotting. Renew it quick sharpish if it is because it will have a detrimental effect on the fabric of the house. You can also opt for a modern compound type of cladding, which should last longer than wood. Pebbledash exteriors are quite unpopular these days and can look better painted. But you do need to make sure the render is sound, because if any is pulling away you could get a damp issue. It can also be removed, but it is quite a costly procedure so will depend on your budget and the market as to whether it's worth it.

Porches

If an unsightly 'stuck on' porch needs changing, it's really worth adding to your 'to do' list. It's all about that first impression, and if it's outdated, or in any way dilapidated, you would be cheating yourself out of your property's top selling price. Building a porch when there isn't one is maybe more of a luxury and therefore not so necessary. If the house needs some character adding to the front and you have the budget for it, this is a clever way to make it more attractive though.

Garden

You can save a lot of money on your refurb by not going too crazy in the garden. Unless it's your real passion, you don't have to make it something worthy of Chelsea Flower Show. As long as it's tidy, with nothing broken, potential buyers are likely to want to put their own stamp on it. Make sure any decking or slabs are level and weeded. It doesn't necessarily have to be ultra-modern unless that suits the property, but it does need to look in good order. When you come to sell, if not before, you could always invest in a few pots

Garden before landscaping

Landscaped garden with different zones

of colourful flowers (colourful at the time you're selling that is!), which you can then take to the next project.

For larger gardens, zoning works well with dedicated areas for eating, lounging and sunbathing. You may need to see the property in different seasons for a full year before deciding where these are best suited. If you have a room looking out onto a patio or garden it's a great idea to have sliding or bifolding doors to make the outdoor area feel like an extension of your indoor living space. A great way to achieve this is by lining the internal area with greenery as well, so that it flows through.

Improving the energy efficiency

When you sell a property you always have to have an energy performance certificate. So improving it is likely to raise the value of your home – and this is becoming increasingly important. Personally, I'm a big believer that it's our duty to make our homes as energy efficient as is affordable anyway. It's worth doing some research as you may find that energy companies are offering incentives so some of the following treatments may be discounted or even free. There may even be government grants you can apply for. You will probably find that many of these are cheaper to do when you're already making improvements to the property, so are worth considering from the start. Here are the ways in which you can up your rating:

- Insulate your roof
- Insulate wall cavities
- Replace older lighting with energy efficient versions
- Replace your boiler
- Use modern devices to control the temperature, like room thermostats or thermostatic radiator valves
- Buy general appliances with higher energy ratings
- Insulate or double-glaze windows and doors
- Add solar panels
- Use a water-saving showerhead

Once all your improvements are made, sit back and give yourself a big pat on the back...then plan the next phase!

PART 3:

SELLING YOUR HOME

CHAPTER 15:
Preparing to sell your home

When to sell

Make sure you are always one step ahead, keeping your eye on your strategy for moving up the property ladder. If your circumstances are likely to change, don't leave it to the last minute to make your move. Although you will have hopefully made a profit on your home, if it's possible for you to save money along the way, to add to your next deposit or to fund the next lot of improvements, it will obviously jet propel your rise up the ladder.

Within reason, you should be able to move as soon as you know you will get a better price for your home. Don't forget to factor into your decision any potential early mortgage repayment penalties. If this is your only or main property and you have shown some kind of permanence living there, you should not be liable to pay capital gains tax. This means any profit made is yours to invest in your next home. There is lack of clarity regarding the amount of time you need to live somewhere to benefit from private residence tax relief though. HMRC look at actual evidence, so accountants I have spoken to advise clients to physically live in a property for at least 12 consecutive months, making sure they have utility bills and are on the Electoral Register for the full term. Seek current advice on this because rules may change. If your circumstances are more complicated you should sit down with a property tax adviser to find out where you stand.

The state of the market shouldn't have a huge influence on your timing, as when you are buying as well as selling it's really a case of swings and roundabouts. If you choose to wait for a seller's market you may not do as well with the property you are buying. Of course, if you choose a buyer's market you may not do so well with how much you sell yours for. Part of your strategy may be to sell in a seller's market and rent until it changes, but you need to have a very solid plan in place. If your financial situation is such that you can buy your next place and keep the current one to rent out, it obviously makes sense to do so during a buyer's market. Because I have always tended to buy properties nobody else seems to want, it's always made sense for me to sell in a seller's market when demand for that property is high, but competition is comparatively low. Of course I've made sure mine is presented in such a way that I blow the competition out of the water anyway!

Preparing for marketing

Whether or not you've had the chance to live in the property for long it needs to *look* like it's just been refurbished in order to reach its top potential price. Once you start talking to agents it can all move very quickly, plus when it is being valued you want to make sure your house looks like the house you will be selling.

Have a good clear out of anything you no longer need as you want it to feel as spacious and as blank a canvas as possible. You don't want ANY clutter. I actually would go as far as to remove all family photos as these are too personal and hinder a potential buyer's ability to imagine themselves in the house. You also want to strip the place of any overtly coloured items to get back to neutral. The idea is not to put anyone off, and as I pointed out earlier, colour can be very divisive. Sell or send to charity shops the belongings you no longer need or want and find somewhere to store those you will take with you. Don't hide things in cupboards or under the beds, because house hunters can be very nosey (me especially!).

Don't be tempted to store things in the loft or garage either because these are important areas to show off – if they're filled to the rafters (literally) with old Christmas decorations, you won't be showing them at their best. Do you have a friend or relative who is happy to keep hold of your 'extras' whilst you sell your place? If not, it's probably worth putting it all into storage. By 'extras', I mean anything you feel you could live without for the next six months or so, including furniture. Trust me, this will really make a difference to the success of viewings.

If there are any marks on walls they either need touch ups or a new coat of paint. Any kind of scuffs can really make a place look and feel shabby.

Dressing your home

House dressing for selling is big business in the States these days, but it's definitely catching on here. There's a good reason for it too. No matter what your estate agent may say when it comes to valuations, human beings can be very visually guided and not always so good at visualizing. I believe it *does* make a big difference to how much you can get for a property. In fact I've proved it many times over. We get very used to our surroundings and can't see (or smell) what others might. As homely as your house or flat may have become, you need to remove yourself from it and start to see it as a product you are looking to market. Remember hundreds of thousands of pounds depend on that shift in thinking. Your home needs to be clutter free, but with a little bit of personality left. It needs to also be immaculately tidy and when people come to viewings it must be spotlessly clean too.

When you are having your photos taken, make sure gear like dog baskets, cat litter trays and big bulky kiddy toys are removed. These items could lead potential buyers to think 'ooh that's not very me' before you even get them through the door. There was one property I sold and the next owner tried to sell it five years later and couldn't even get the same price for it. The market hadn't gone down so this didn't really make sense. So I had a look at their photos and it was immediately obvious to me. Firstly, they had pine furniture in odd places, which stuck out like sore thumbs against the white décor. Secondly, they had purple cushions and a purple rug – they clearly really liked purple, but unfortunately many people don't. The most surprising to me was it looked like they hadn't even tidied for the photos. There were kids' toys all over the place. A pile of post and other bits and pieces like loose change and sunglasses were left on surfaces. I know these are items we live with on a day-to-day basis but they should just go into a drawer for the photos and viewings.

Lots of plants are a must, faux ones will do as long as they look realistic – cheap, obviously fake ones will do your home no favours. Vases of flowers also give a fresh, vibrant look to a room. Photographers for home magazines always bring floral displays to dress rooms so follow their lead.

You want nothing broken in the house. Even a single cracked tile can be off-putting so get it replaced. Rid your bathroom and windows of any mould, even if it means redoing the grouting or sealant.

Arrange your furniture so that it makes sense, but also gives an open feel to a room. You have hopefully already removed and put into storage any unnecessary pieces that might make a room feel small or awkward.

If a room is being sold as a bedroom, make sure it looks like a bedroom – even if it means buying a cheap bed to make it obvious. Certainly don't let it be viewed as a dumping ground or an office, because if someone is looking for a 3-bedroom house, they want to *feel* like it's a 3-bedroom house without too much imagination.

Make sure the garden is neat and tidy, with any dead plants trimmed back, the lawn mowed and patio jet-washed. If you haven't already, it's worth setting up a little seating zone, just a bistro table and chairs will do. Outdoor living is very important to people and if you are lucky enough to have outside space it's a big selling point, so make the most of it.

I'm really hoping I don't need to tell you to make beds and plump up cushions. I did once view a house where the beds looked like they'd just been slept in. In the teenage boy's room the sheets were disgusting and the room smelled of...well teenage boys unsurprisingly! It led me to think 'these people aren't worried about what price they will get for this place so I am going to get a bargain' and sure enough I had no competition when putting in an offer.

It's a good idea to get a free-speaking friend around to get their opinion. It's quite hard to be subjective about your own home and others are likely to see what you will miss. If you really feel you need some help in this department and don't trust your own judgment, it is worth employing a professional house dresser. I am certain that presenting your house in the right way massively affects the price you get for it.

The advice above is just for the photos – there's more to come on preparing for viewings!

Deciding how much your property is worth

No matter how or who is going to sell your home, you need to be one step ahead of the valuation. These days it's very easy to compare properties and their prices because of the numerous Internet sites available. These are only guestimates though, and the first thing you need to do is update the likes of Zoopla and other portals so that the online valuation reflects the fact that this is a very different property to the one you bought. Then you want to look at similar properties in the area that have been sold recently and how much they have gone for.

Get at least three agents around to give their opinion on the value of the house. I say at least three because I have encountered wildly different ones for the same property at the same time. Bear in mind that some agents work by the strategy of going above what they think it is worth to win your business, but will then come to you when it hasn't sold within a few weeks to say you need to drop the price. At the other end of the spectrum, some agents just want a quick sale so go low knowing it will fly off the shelf and they get their commission faster. Of course the difference in their commission is pennies compared to what *you* miss out on if you undersell. With one property the gap between the top and bottom valuations I received on a £600k property was £100k. The property sold within four days at the top price, compared with a very similar house on the same road that sold for £500k.

One thing to bear in mind, which you need to keep an eye on from the moment you buy and improve your property, is how close you are to the next stamp duty bracket. If you tip over the edge it is going to be much more difficult to sell above it as the buyer will have to pay so much more tax.

Sell your property yourself?

As much as I love DIY, this is taking it a step too far. I have spoken to people who swear they don't need any kind of agent. Well one of the key reasons to use one is that the likes of Rightmove and Zoopla will only deal with verified agents. If you're not on these online portals you are going to struggle to reach even a fraction of house-hunters. I would say put it in the hands of someone who knows what they're doing, but always remember you are the client.

Choosing an estate agent

If you don't have much spare time and you hate the idea of conducting viewings and negotiating, the best way to sell your home is through a traditional high street agent. They need to be in the right market for your home as some agencies only deal with certain types of property, so are specialists in that field. Feel free to do some undercover work and pose as a potential buyer to see how you find the service they give. Getting a recommendation is a good idea, but talk to as many as you can to find someone you feel you trust and can communicate with. If you're not keen on the valuation they give, because it doesn't tally with your thorough research, you should be able to have a conversation with them without feeling bullied into submission.

An agent will generally charge a fee as a percentage of the value of the house. They will take photos, create floorplans, organise your Energy Performance Certificate, advertise, arrange and conduct viewings, check the funds of any buyer making offers to ensure they are serious, negotiate the sale and do their best to push it through by liaising with solicitors and other agents where there is a chain. They will often ask for exclusivity, but this is negotiable – you tend to pay a higher fee for non-exclusivity though. Their fee might also be flexible – particularly with the rise of online agents. I know someone who has always approached agents with the line 'This is the amount I will pay you to sell my house' and it's worked for him! If your property has a lot of competition though, bear in mind that if their incentive to sell it is diminished they may push the other properties more than yours. Having said that, you should always haggle! Make sure you thoroughly read all the Ts & Cs before signing anything as you need to know how long you will be tied into using them.

It's important you are happy with the chosen photos and information on the particulars. Yes agents should be experienced in what sells houses, but in busy times they may miss out vital pieces of information, so proof-read the details before they are printed. Remember nobody knows your home as well as you do.

You need to be reviewing their performance regularly and they should also be on top of giving you feedback from viewings. Make sure you are very much available and that they would be able to get hold of you at all times, or at least within half an hour of calling, as this will make everyone's lives easier when arranging viewings. Also be prepared to put yourself out to allow visits whenever necessary. If a potential buyer can't get an appointment, they may lose interest or find something else before they even get the chance to view yours. If you have any doubts about your agent's performance, just move on as soon as you are able, as the last thing you want is for your house to be on the market unsold for too long.

Online agents

I have used online agents with great success actually and saved a fortune in the process. I can't speak for all the online businesses out there, as there are so many these days, but I found the viewings booking service to be a dream, which has meant more footfall and at a faster pace. Many have booking representatives available in the evenings, which is a big plus considering most people want to be able to call up and book a viewing when they are not at work.

The online agents tend to charge a flat rate, which ends up significantly cheaper (particularly with higher value homes). Some will conduct viewings as well, but I actually like the idea of doing these myself as no one would know my property as well as I do, and have such a vested interest in selling it. This works for me as I am very comfortable talking to people and am not likely to take any negative reactions to heart. Bear in mind though that if you go down this route and you aren't the right person for the job you could hinder the sale and the price. High street agents, for example, prefer the vendor not to be present as they feel they can glean more honest feedback from those viewing the property and then alleviate any concerns they have to get them interested again.

Most online agents do offer the same service as high street agents, but there's a chance they won't be specialists in your local area, and are unlikely to have the same kind of relationships with the local community. People do still pop in to high street agents when they're passing by as well, which is of course a service online agencies cannot offer. It can save a fortune though so is definitely worth considering if you're confident in your sales and negotiation techniques.

To do list

- Clear clutter and sell or donate to charity. Find somewhere to store anything else
- Refresh walls
- Fix anything that is broken
- Dress rooms appropriately
- Remove any personal items like photos, kids' toys, pet paraphernalia
- Update online portals so they take into account the improvements you have made
- Arrange for at least three agent valuations
- Do your own research on the value of your property
- Choose your agent and read the contract thoroughly
- Make sure the particulars include all selling points

CHAPTER 16:
Getting the place sold quickly

Help to sell your home

Firstly, tell EVERYONE you are looking to sell. I just don't know why anyone ever chooses not to have a 'For Sale' sign outside their house. Some fear they might upset the neighbours, but you are going to have to tell them at some point and you never know, they might have someone in mind they want to be their new neighbour. Who knows, they may even be happy to see you go!!! So make sure it's the first thing you tell anyone you meet, as word of mouth is a powerful way to get a message out there. Take it one step further even and go onto local forums – particularly the mums and dads ones, as you could cast your net even wider. You could also advertise in the local paper, but statistics show that most people search the Internet portals these days.

You could be really proactive and identify properties that your potential buyers are likely to be moving from and drop leaflets through their letterboxes. This may just give them the incentive they need to get moving!

Preparing your home for viewings

Hopefully most of the hard work has been done before you had your photos taken. Remember to follow all the same rules when people come round to view your home, as litter trays and the like have probably started to resurface since your initial clear-out.

You need to clean, clean and clean again. The place needs to be spotless. Even wash the front door and jet wash the drive so you get that all-important first impression right. Glass screens in bathrooms, windows and mirrors all need to be immaculate. Make sure plants don't have any dead bits and flowers are fresh. If you have any pulls in the carpet snip them off so they don't draw attention. If the carpet isn't brand new, shampoo it. Oil squeaky doors so the place feels fresh and new.

There's the old advice to have bread baking and coffee brewing, but it's almost so clichéd I think people are probably a little suspicious when someone has gone down this route. It is important the place smells good though. You might not realize that it doesn't usually because you're used to it! Don't go for cheap air fresheners though as they smell tacky and can even cause allergies. I actually think it's quite a nice idea to have a couple of strategically placed expensive candles or room fresheners. Your home will then smell good but also have the air of quality about it.

On that note, unless you have a really swanky car, park well away. You want people to imagine the kind of life they will have living there and an old banger or even a mediocre car points their imagination in the wrong direction. It's not about deception but perception. I've known people to even rent a Mercedes to park in their drive for viewings, but I think that's taking things a little too far!

All lights, including side lamps should be on, even during the daytime so it looks as big and light as possible. Make sure the house is warm enough. I've never heard of people not buying a house because it was too warm, but a cold house will definitely put potential buyers off – particularly if they are reptiles like me!

Ask that people take their shoes off when they enter so they can see you are looking after their potential future home.

Dealing with viewings

You may have decided that you are going to show potential buyers around. Or it may be that the agent wants you to make yourself scarce for viewings. It may be *you* want to make yourself scarce because you can't think of anything worse than being there when people are judging your home! It may be that the odd potential buyer can only come when an agent or viewing assistant isn't available so you end up on duty anyway. As I have conducted many viewings myself, here are my tips to help things run smoothly:

✓ Practise what you're going to say beforehand. Imagine you are the potential buyer and the kinds of questions you would be asking and have the answers ready.

✓ Visualise it all going really well. This can really help to calm the nerves and give you confidence.

✓ SMILE! Sounds funny, but when a person's nervous they can come across as miserable or aloof, which will create a cold atmosphere.

✓ There's no need to tell them every minute detail, but it is worth pointing out that a lot of work has been put into the house so that when they see how much you bought it for they understand why the price has risen faster than the market.

✓ Be careful not to give them too much information about how it was when you bought it. I made the mistake of telling people at a viewing that the previous owner had been a heavy smoker as I was trying to make sure they knew this was a very different house to the one I had paid a fraction of the price I was asking for. I had stripped it out so I knew there wasn't even the faintest smell of cigarettes, but even me mentioning it led one woman to write in her feedback that she could still smell it!

✓ Less is more generally. Let them ask the questions, rather than you tell them information they don't necessarily need.

✓ When you've shown them around once, say you will leave them to have a look independently so they don't feel like you're looking over their shoulders. This is their opportunity to imagine themselves living there so you want to get out of the way. Even go outside so they can chat if they are a couple.

✓ Answer their questions as honestly as you can. There's no point in lying, as the truth will come out further down the line.

✓ Whatever you do, don't ask them what they think of it, which will make them feel incredibly uncomfortable and even put them off returning for a second viewing.

✓ If they don't seem very interested you mustn't take it personally. They may even love it, but don't want to seem overly keen!

Open house viewings

I thought it was worth mentioning these as it has become more popular these days for agents to recommend open house viewings.

The great thing about these is if they are successful you will get a load of potential buyers across the threshold in one go and will only have to tidy up the once! If you have pets and/or kids and the open house is over a weekend it might even be worth all staying at a friend's for the night.

An open house situation can put you in the driving seat as a vendor as it creates a buzz and sends out a message that there's a lot of interest and people need to move quickly and bid against each other. It can put some people off though as they would prefer to take their time about it. You could also miss potential buyers who aren't able to make it and what's to say they wouldn't have put in a higher offer? So there are pros and cons for you to weigh up if your agent suggests this as an option.

To do list

- Tell EVERYONE you are selling!
- Spread the word via online forums
- Repeat the clearing out process you did for the photos
- Make sure the house is immaculately tidy
- Clean, clean and clean again (even your front door!)
- Fill the house with fresh flowers
- Burn high quality scented candles
- Practise your questions and answers if you will be doing your viewings

CHAPTER 17:
Accepting an offer to moving day

Accepting an offer

Quite often a second and even third viewing takes place before an offer is made. You can consider them an interested party if they come back a second time, but it certainly doesn't mean it's a done deal. If someone makes an offer after a first viewing, alarm bells ring for me as I fear the price may be too low and they want to snap it up and take it off the market.

I'm also very wary if an agent manages to secure a sale before even putting it to market. This often happens if they have an investor in mind. First of all, if someone is seeing this as a potential business opportunity they are not going to want to pay top dollar for it, but also I want to test the market a bit rather than settle for the first person that comes along. The way I look at it is I certainly wasn't going to marry the first boy I ever dated!

When an offer does come through don't get carried away with excitement. If you know it to be a fair offer and the situation of the buyer is sound, you can still make them wait! An offer being made is only an early hurdle so stay calm and in control. If the offer is too low it is down to you or your agent to go back to them and tell them so. I've always had the mind-set that unless I get the price I think it is worth I am not budging, which is why I avoid finding the next place before selling mine so I am in no hurry to sell. An agent will often give an indication as to what the vendor would probably accept. This is obviously harder to do when you are negotiating directly.

Once an offer is accepted, the buyer will usually ask for the property to come off the market and for any further viewings to be cancelled. It will now be posted as 'sold', 'sale agreed', 'under offer', or 'sold subject to contract'. Make sure you always keep the details of interested parties in case the sale falls through at any point.

The next step will be for the buyer to arrange any necessary surveys and then the lawyers get involved.

You might also want to start looking for your next place, if you haven't already. It's not happened yet, but if I get a good offer on a property, I am always prepared to rent in the interim, rather than be put under undue stress to find somewhere within the timeframe required by my buyer. There are a couple of reasons for this. Firstly, I don't want to make rash decisions when it comes to spending that much money. Secondly, if unscrupulous buyers get a whiff of desperation they might be tempted to find something wrong with the property and reduce their offer at crunch time and push you into a corner. Buyers have tried that with me and ended up with egg on their faces as I stood firm. Thirdly, if I can't find what I want and end up having to rent, I become chain-free, which could even put me in good stead for getting a better price for the place I'm buying. Yes there is more hassle, admin and rental costs involved, but look at the figures to see if it is worth it.

We talked earlier about 'gazundering' in Chapter 8, so you now need to know how to avoid being put in this position. If you find yourself with a number of interested parties, things are always likely to move more quickly with a chain-free buyer. Setting an early exchange date and always encouraging everyone to move quickly to complete can also help to avoid being gazundered. The longer the process lasts the more likely it is to collapse. It's also a good idea to build a positive relationship with your buyer. Both solicitors and agents don't always like this, but once it becomes personal it does make it harder for them to pull a swift one!

The conveyancing process

Oh we are nowhere near done yet I'm afraid. Now we enter the very frustrating world of conveyancing again, which is even worse when you are selling – particularly if you are buying at the same time. Make sure you get a good one through referrals, or perhaps tested out yourself when you were buying. Your agent may have one he or she can recommend as well, which can actually be a good idea as they are more likely to work together to make the sale happen if they are chums.

I have literally felt like I'm banging my head against a brick wall when dealing with poor conveyancing teams. One actually got the house I was buying mixed up with the house I was selling. Yep that really filled me with confidence, as you can imagine!

One of the big frustrations for me has been the drip-feeding of requests for standard documents. Now if you have followed my lead through this book you should have neatly filed all necessary paperwork so this will hopefully not be too laborious a task now you need to dig them out. Here is a list of what you need to get ready:

Proof of identity
Passport or driving license and a utility bill with the seller's name from the past three months are needed.

Title deeds
If you have a mortgage, the lender will have the deeds in safe storage. You will need to give your solicitor the mortgage account number so they can obtain a redemption statement in preparation for completion.

Property information forms
There are two different ones. The first one details everything that is to be included in the sale of the property – fixtures, fittings, white goods and even furnishings if it has been agreed with the buyer. They may wish to buy certain items like curtains or blinds, for example, so you should have settled on a price for these. Check through it with a fine toothed comb as you know better than your solicitor what is to be included.

The second will ask for the following:

- Boundaries
- Alterations, planning and building control (this applies to anything you have done to the property but also for work done by previous owners. You should have all of this from when you

bought the house. If there are any issues, insurance can be taken out against future problems arising.

- Guarantees and warranties (absolutely anything you have a warranty for that will remain in the property, especially new windows and boilers).
- Insurance details (may be asked out of interest).
- Any disputes or complaints.
- Notices and proposals (neighbours or local authorities).
- Rights and any informal arrangements (quite often refers to shared access issues).
- Details of any off-road parking.
- Other charges (lease expenses or management fees, usually for flats or private roads/estates).
- Details of any environmental matters (like flooding in the area).
- Occupiers (this is in relation to rental properties where a tenant will be staying on).
- Situation of seller and any agreed completion/moving dates.
- State of utilities at the property (wiring, heating and plumbing. Make sure you have your boiler service certificates).
- Utilities and services connections (gas, electricity, water and location of relevant meters).

Leasehold Information Form
This is obviously only relevant for leasehold properties. It confirms to whom the seller pays rent and service charges. There will also be details about responsibilities for the common areas and also any building works the seller was liable for.

Most recent utility bills
A buyer may wish to see these, so it's worth having them ready.

Leasehold or shared freehold documents

Energy performance certificate
Your agent should have arranged for an accredited assessor to carry this out.

Once the solicitors have agreed the draft contract between them, it will be sent to both the seller and buyer to check. At this stage, if your solicitor is pro-active he/she will also send out a Transfer TR1 document, which tells Land Registry to change the owner of the property in the property's legal documents. Doing this now saves the common mad panic at the end of the process, so it might be worth asking them if this has been done! Once both parties have agreed, the final contract will be sent for you to sign.

Now that all sounds straightforward doesn't it? The reality is though that either party might need things to slow down when there's a chain. The problem is you will often be left in the dark wondering why things aren't moving at your pace. Keep talking to your solicitor as they should know everything that is happening, and should actually be keeping you posted even when there is no news. If your agent is helping to chase, inform your solicitor of this too as they need to be kept in the loop. The reality is you have little control over things other than to pull out altogether. As long as you are doing everything on your side as promptly as possible you need to try and remain calm, as stress can mount otherwise. If you are also buying another property and the delay is putting that purchase at risk, then your agent should be making it clear to all parties that the chain is in danger of breaking, which often has the desired effect of speeding things up!

But chains do break I'm afraid, and it can feel very dispiriting that you are back to square one. If this happens, take a deep breath and remind yourself that nobody is dying here. If you miss out on a property you were looking to buy, you never know, it might be for the best. If I had a penny for every story I've heard of people saying things turned out better in the end after a sale fell through, well I'd be investing it in property!

Next you need to exchange contracts, which may or may not be on the same day as completion, depending on what both parties have agreed. Keys are only handed over once you complete though and the funds from your seller have been received.

Moving day

Phew we got there! Remember again to take all meter readings and transfer/cancel accounts. Refer back to the earlier chapter for advice on packing and moving admin. Make sure you leave your property clean and tidy as a token of goodwill. You shouldn't leave anything behind that wasn't in the agreement otherwise your buyer could charge you to have it removed. It's always better to leave a home on a sweet note – besides it's good to get those karma points to help you as you climb that ladder.

Enjoy your homes along the way, and at times you may want and need to stay put for longer than you'd like, but until you're in that forever home always keep your eye on the next step. Best of luck, please do let me know how you get on and remember Churchill's words; "Success is not final, failure is not fatal. It is the courage to continue that counts."

To do list

- **Instruct your solicitor**
- **Dig out all necessary documents**
- **Make sure you have time to respond immediately**
- **Keep calm!**
- **Read the earlier chapter again to help with packing**
- **Take meter readings and transfer or cancel accounts**
- **Make sure all necessary items have been packed**
- **Clean the property**
- **Make sure your stamp duty has been paid**
- **Enjoy this next step closer to your forever home!**
- **Let me know how you get on**

About the author

I wanted to explain further about my background and what has driven me, so you can understand where I'm coming from. Neither my husband nor I grew up with a silver spoon in our mouths. Many hear my accent and assume I had my own pony as a child. My father in fact came from the Australian equivalent to a council estate. Against all the odds he managed to train as an accountant. We started life in Sydney – I was born there. It wasn't expensive like it is now, and my parents were able to buy a small place, although far out from the centre and from where my father worked. We lived next door to a couple that had parties every night and whose Rottweiler attacked my three-year-old brother. You get the picture.

My parents actually did very well on that property. They didn't have a deposit so got a cheeky loan for 'furnishings' but used it as a down-payment for a mortgage and made or bought everything from charity shops instead. I love a story of an upcycled divan bed they made into sofa! They bought the house for $35,000. They transformed it from ruined to respectable, using their limited DIY skills, and sold it for $145,000. Do you know what is really interesting is that I only learned this when writing this book – but it goes to show I was brought up by parents with the attitude I am hoping to pass onto you.

They emigrated to the UK, on my mum's insistence as she was not happy there. I was bullied at school because of my Aussie accent and so mum made sure I adopted a plummy one instead! It was always going to be tough, even as an extremely hard working accountant, for my father to ever become very wealthy. His qualification wasn't particularly respected in the UK at the time because it was from Australia. He didn't have a degree – my brothers and I were the first to go to University in our family. He also didn't want to work for a London firm as he preferred to live on the south coast so he could surf. My English mother came from a slightly wealthier background, but disowned her father when her parents split up, so any wealth didn't trickle down.

Having done well on that Sydney property, my parents did manage to buy a bungalow though, which in time they extended from two to four bedrooms. The following house they also did up, although they never quite got around to replacing the hideous orange kitchen. They encountered financial problems with a business venture and they found it necessary to move down a step. Unfortunately their marriage also started to break down at this stage. I always say my parents divorced over an orange kitchen!!! There was one more move before they actually would part ways, and again they did extensive work to that house.

Each time I had a big hand in styling and decorating my bedrooms. By the time we moved to this final house I was a teenager. I was told that under NO circumstances was I allowed to strip the carpet and sand the floorboards. One day, I rolled back the carpet, hired a sander and sanded the floorboards whilst my parents were out, and it took them weeks to notice. I guess my teenage rebellion was slightly different to others! My parents split in that house. I also parted ways from my father as ours was not a very harmonious relationship. Several years later my mother had to sell the house because she couldn't afford the mortgage. So many bad things happened in that home, but I still look back at it so fondly because I loved its character, and I ruddy loved that bedroom! As far as I know my father has rented ever since.

When I went to University I would take great care to decorate my rooms. I even stayed up three days and nights in a row to finish one. We then had to move just weeks later because it was so damp! I was at Warwick University so had many wealthy friends who would pay me to style their rooms. I couldn't believe my luck as although I was studying English Literature, interior design was my real passion. I much preferred doing this to listening to Germaine Greer talk about Shakespeare!

When I moved to London on graduating, I would put in great effort to style each and every room I rented. And I rented a great many different rooms! At the age of 27 I met my now husband. When we were moving in together we both wanted to get more for our money than we would be able to in London. After watching an episode of 'Location, Location, Location' we decided to try Folkestone. We spent a weekend there and fell in love with it. We rented at first and then bought a basement flat in an Edwardian building for £70k. It was very shabby, but it was ours. We put a lot of love and care into doing that place up with our own hands. All the furniture was bought second-hand, or found on the roadside and upcycled. We then sold this property a couple of years later for £120k, the price of a 2-bed flat, and the buyer also bought every item of furniture I'd upcycled. This was when I realised I had a knack for it.

Over the years, I managed to find houses nobody else seemed to want, do them up on a reasonable budget, but without cutting corners, and then sell them for a strong market price. This was always whilst working and doing tiring shift patterns. There have been many lows. Christmases confined to a bedroom because it was the only dust-free room, and months at a time without a bathroom because it was ripped out at the start of a project and not replaced until the end (a tough but important lesson to learn – don't let the builders do anything without talking it through first!). The most gruelling time though has been during the most recent project: doing up a 3000-square-foot, nearly derelict house whilst having my first baby. I only took about a week's maternity leave, mainly because I was in hospital for most of that time due to complications. The minute I was out, I was choosing colours and project managing in place of an absent builder!

We had to rent during our recent project because it was in such a state we couldn't live there. Instead, I would use my daughter's nap times to go over to the house and make sure the guys were doing what they should be doing. I would feed her at 7pm and come over and expose brickwork and scrape paint off banisters by the light of a mobile phone because there was no electricity...and then get back for the 10pm feed. It was hard work. It was worth it though. It meant that I went from owning a 1-bed flat in Folkestone to a forever home in Sevenoaks in 8 years. I hope that this demonstrates that by replicating what I've done you can move up that ladder and live where you want to in time.

In a nutshell, unless you are very wealthy you will need to play the long game. It is unlikely that your first, or even your second home will be big, shiny and in the ideal location. It's time to reassess your priorities and spending habits. But from the start you will be working towards that dream home in the dream location, and it's that light at the end of the tunnel that will keep you going. Boy does it feel good when you reach it.

To help others to do the same I started combining my skills as a TV presenter (BBC weather, Sky, Channel 5), home coach (helping others to improve their homes) and property developer a couple of years ago by producing a vlog and blog TheHomeGenie.com. The feedback has been overwhelming, and I've loved the sharing of ideas, but also hearing inspiring stories. I felt this book would be a neat way to have all the experience I've learned in one place.

I hope you've enjoyed the book and found my guidance useful. Please do let me know your thoughts and I'd love to hear about your own experiences and successes. You can contact me through www.TheHomeGenie.com.

Georgina Burnett, Kent, December 2018